BRADFORD W.G. PUBLIC LIBRARY

P9-DOA-198

BRADFORD W/G LIBRARY
100 HOLLAND COURT BOX 130
BRADFORD ONT. L3Z 2A7

ESSENTIAL
ANNUALS

ESSENTIAL
ANNUALS

The 100 Best for Design and Cultivation

Text by Elizabeth Murray • Photography by Derek Fell

CRESCENT BOOKS
NEW YORK

DISCARDED
BRADFORD WG
PUBLIC LIBRARY

BRADFORD WG LIBRARY
100 HOLLAND COURT, BOX 130
BRADFORD, ONT. L3Z 2A7

A FRIEDMAN GROUP BOOK

This 1989 edition published by Crescent Books
distributed by Crown Publishers, Inc.
225 Park Avenue South
New York, New York 10003

Copyright © 1989 by Michael Friedman Publishing Group, Inc.

All rights reserved. No part of this publication may be reproduced, stored in a retrieval
system, or transmitted, in any form or by any means, electronic, photocopying, recording,
or otherwise, without the prior written permission of the publisher.

Library of Congress Cataloging-in-Publication Data

Essential annuals
p.   cm.

ISBN 0-517-66177-2

1. Annuals (Plants)   2. Annual (Plants)—Pictorial Works.
3. Gardens—Designs and plans.   I. Crescent Books.
SB422.E77   1989   88-21734
716—dc19   CIP

ESSENTIAL ANNUALS: The 100 Best for Design and Cultivation
was prepared and produced by
Michael Friedman Publishing Group, Inc.
15 West 26th Street
New York, New York 10010

Editor: Sharon Kalman
Art Director/Designer: Robert W. Kosturko
Photo Editor: Christopher Bain
Production Manager: Karen Greenberg
Layout/Illustrations: Alanna M. Georgens

Typeset by Mar+x Myles Graphics, Inc.
Color separated, printed, and bound by South Sea International Press, Ltd.

h g f e d c b a

DEDICATION

To my three sisters who love flowers—Mary, Cathy, and Pam

ACKNOWLEDGMENTS

Special love and thanks to my friends Susan, Barbara, Beth, Ellie, Kay, and Janet.

Table of Contents

9   INTRODUCTION

Instant Color, Continuous Bloom

13   CHAPTER ONE

Annual Basics

BUYING QUALITY TRANSPLANTS
SOIL PREPARATION FOR ANNUALS
SITE SELECTION, IRRIGATION, AND AFTER CARE
GROWING ANNUALS IN CONTAINERS

27   CHAPTER TWO

The Encyclopedia of Essential Annuals

85   **CHAPTER THREE**

Garden Plans
ISLAND BED; RECTANGLE
"COLONIAL" FORMAL GARDEN; WILLIAMSBURG DESIGN
"FRENCH" FORMAL GARDEN; DIAMOND DESIGN
"ENGLISH" FORMAL GARDEN; CARTWHEEL DESIGN
BUTTERFLY GARDEN (TO ATTRACT BUTTERFLIES)

119   **CHAPTER FOUR**
PLANT SELECTION GUIDE

132   **APPENDIX**
ANNUAL FLOWERING GUIDE

138   **SOURCES**

140   **INDEX OF BOTANICAL AND COMMON NAMES**

This all-white theme garden features white- and cream-colored annuals, including varieties of hibiscus, zinnnia, and euphorbia.

INTRODUCTION

INSTANT COLOR, CONTINUOUS BLOOM

COMPARED TO OTHER TYPES OF ORNAMENtal plants, flowering annuals provide an abundance of bloom quickly, but all for a minimal investment of time and money. They are the easiest flowering plants to grow—far more dependable than perennials, flowering bulbs, and flowering shrubs. A packet of seeds costing a dollar or less can produce thousands of plants. Even if you prefer to let a professional bedding plant grower start the seeds for you, and buy transplants from a garden center, it's possible to purchase annuals for as little as twenty-five cents each when you buy them in flats.

Many people feel a much greater sense of accomplishment when they grow their own annuals from seed. To see how easy it can be—even with small seeds—turn to page 13 where a variety of seed starting techniques are presented.

Annuals are undemanding plants that can be fully grown in one season, usually flowering within six to twelve weeks from the time they are sown. Depending on the climate you live in and the varieties you choose, annuals can produce a bold, brilliant floral display lasting from four weeks to seven months. A large selection of young plants already in flower is available from local garden centers in early spring, so the impatient gardener can add instant color to the garden.

It is amazing how versatile annuals can be. Displays of annuals can be used exclusively in beds and borders; they can be mixed with perennials to fill the gaps of a perennial border, offering color continuity as the perennials come in and out of bloom; and many annuals can be planted in containers, especially hanging baskets, making it possible even for city gardeners to decorate confined areas and hard-to-plant spaces like balconies, terraces, and patios. For more information about container gardening, see page 21.

Some annuals—like marigolds and snapdragons—are so versatile that they grow in every state, from Florida to Alaska to Hawaii. Whether you have cool or hot summers, rich or poor soil, moist or dry soil, sun or shade, you will find a wide range of annuals to fit every need of your garden and produce a colorful display. The lists starting on page 119 will help you choose the right varieties for your particular needs.

Whatever your garden design requirements, there are annuals to meet them. Annuals that creep along the ground, such as alyssum and *Zinnia angustifolia* (Classic zinnia), are suitable to use as ground-cover plants, and they have an added bonus of flowers; annuals that stand tall and erect, such as cleome and sunflowers, are suitable for backgrounds and structural highlights; annuals that cascade and spill over the edges, such as lobelia and petunias, are suitable for raised beds, pots, and balconies; annuals with long stems are suitable for cutting so you can fill your home with fresh flowers, many with the added attraction of a pleasant fragrance. Again, the lists starting on page 119 will provide specific information.

Perhaps the biggest advantage of annuals is their extensive color range, making them suitable for creative garden designs, particularly gardens of a single color theme, such as "white gardens," "golden gardens," "blue gardens," and even "green gardens." Gardens that cover large expanses can emulate the French Renaissance style of "carpet bedding," in which generous swatches of color are planted in swirls and flourishes, or in more formal geometric shapes. The color schemes can be dramatic, using strong colors such as yellow, orange, and red, or subtle and sophisticated, using subdued colors such as blue, white, and pink. To help you devise some effective garden designs using annuals, a number of garden plans are featured, beginning on page 85, with specific planting ideas for both sunny and shady locations.

When planning to include annuals in your garden, don't be put off by garden writers who describe annuals as "boring." Anyone who thinks of them this way hasn't traveled enough and seen annuals displayed in beautiful and imaginative ways. To prove how stimulating and exciting annuals can be, the photographs chosen show a variety of appealing garden uses. Even in the encyclopedia section, the specimens selected are shown as an integral part of a garden.

Opposite page, far left, above: Claude Monet's garden at Giverney, France is famous for its "Grand Allee," featuring annual nasturtiums that creep across a gravel walk way.
Opposite page, far left, below: This fence features a morning glory vine and a border of wax begonias.
Opposite page, left: An effective companion-planting of perennial scarlet sage and annual vinca.

Left: Pansies and alyssum define a serpentine border at a Tucson, Arizona home in early spring.

This mixed border of petunias, marigolds, blue salvia, and spider plants blooms continuously from early summer to fall frost.

CHAPTER ONE

ANNUAL BASICS

THE SEEDS OF MOST ANNUALS ARE extremely easy to germinate, requiring little more than moist potting soil that maintains a temperature of 70°F. Generally speaking, if a seed is tiny—such as begonias and petunias—it should not be completely covered with soil, but pressed into the upper soil surface (just enough to anchor it), since exposure to light improves the rate of germination.

With such fine seeds lying on the soil's surface, it is extremely difficult to prevent them from drying out; a good practice is to enclose the seed-starting unit (see pages 13 to 15) in a plastic bag, away from direct sunlight. The plastic helps create a humid microclimate, allowing moisture to condense on the inner wall, thus keeping the seeds from dehydrating.

Once seedlings are up, they should be watered on a regular basis to keep the soil moist, and placed in a location with bright, constant light. If moisture is infrequent or sunlight comes only from one direction, then the plants will "stretch," producing poor transplants. When growing seedlings on a windowsill, raise the level of the seed-starting unit so the seedlings are closer to the light, and also consider placing a reflector on the side of the seed-starting unit that receives the least amount of light. A handy reflector can be made by simply wrapping aluminum foil around a piece of cardboard and propping it against the unit.

Different varieties of annuals require different periods of time in which to germinate and grow into useful transplants. Slow-growing plants such as begonias may need as many as ten to twelve weeks to be large enough to transplant, while French marigolds can be ready to transplant in four weeks. The seed packet will generally advise you as to how long it should take to start a variety from seed, and whether the variety can tolerate frost (hardy annual) or is killed by frost (tender annual).

A large number of flowering annuals dislike being transplanted and prefer to be sown directly into the garden; Shirley poppies are a good example. However, many people still prefer to start them indoors in order to get earlier blooms in the garden. In this case, it is vital to choose a method of seed starting that prevents root disturbance at transplant time.

Seed-Starting Techniques

Basically, there are two types of seed-starting techniques: the *one-step* and the *two-step*. These two methods (plus two others), as well as information on starting hard-to-start seeds are illustrated for you. In a one-step system the seeds are sown directly into a pot, such as a Jiffy-pot, Jiffy pellet, Fertl-cube, Maxi-pot, or other brands. As the seeds germinate, the seedlings are thinned, leaving just one strong seedling to grow to transplant size. There is no transfer to another pot.

With the two-step method (mostly used with fine-seeded varieties such as begonias and petunias and wherever very large quantities of transplants are desired), the seed is first sown into a seed tray—or a seed flat—either scattered over the entire surface and pressed in, or else sown into furrows made by a straight edge.

The seeds should be allowed to germinate thick and fast (heat from a heating cable under the seed tray will encourage rapid germination), but as soon as they are large enough to handle, the best-looking seedlings should be pulled out gently and transferred to individual pots until they have reached transplant size.

When growing seedlings it is extremely important to use sterile materials—both potting soil and pots. Don't use soil dumped out from other pots or garden soil, and if you are recycling old pots make sure they are thoroughly cleaned

SEED-STARTING METHOD #1

The illustrations on the opposite page show various seed-starting techniques.

1-Scatter seeds thinly over soil surface in seed tray.

2-Thin out seedlings to leave only the healthiest plants.

3-Transfer to individual pots when large enough to handle.

4-Place a group of seeds in the planting hole of a peat pellet.

5-Thin seedlings to a single strong plant.

6-Gently remove netting to free roots at time of transplanting.

with soapy water. This kind of hygiene is extremely important in order to avoid a common fungus disease called "damping-off" that attacks young seedlings. A symptom of this disease is a tendency for the seedling to keel over, weakened at the soil line. As an extra precaution against the disease a fungicide like Benomyl or Benlate can be sprayed over the soil surface of newly seeded containers.

It is also extremely important to subject all seedlings to a period of "hardening-off" before they are transferred from a comfortable indoor environment to a relatively cold, exposed, outdoor environment. The hardening-off process requires several days in a cold frame so that when the transplants finally make the full transition to their garden locations, they can withstand unexpected temperature fluctuations. A cold frame—usually consisting of an aluminum frame with a vented glass top that opens automatically on warm, sunny days so the seedlings don't burn—can be purchased from mail-order garden suppliers and local garden centers. A makeshift cold frame can be easily constructed by using plastic sheeting stretched over wire hoops. Or, seedlings can simply be left in an unheated porch area for several days before going into the garden.

Today, there are many seed-starting units available. Below is an evaluation of each one.

Peat Pellets These consist of compressed peat, and come in two types: the Jiffy-7 peat pellet, the peat being bound together with a plastic netting, and the Jiffy-9 peat pellet, which has no netting and is held together with an invisible "binder." You place both types in a shallow tray of water where they soak up the moisture and expand to several times their original height. They become soft and have a depression in the top for sowing seeds. Both kinds have a tendency to dry out rather quickly unless kept out of direct sunlight and enclosed in plastic bags. Also, plants grown in the Jiffy-7 peat pellets generally do better if the netting is gently removed, otherwise it can inhibit root development. These peat pellets are inexpensive and available in kit form with watering tray and plastic dome included.

Peat Pots These are either square or round. The square pots are joined at the lip, and choosing them over the round pots allows you to fill a large number at a time with potting soil. These pots need to be filled with planting soil and kept

moist. As the plants grow, the roots will actually penetrate the sides of the pot; soon after transplanting, the peat decomposes to give the roots freedom to grow. However, even with this feature of rapidly biodegradable peat sides, it is still a good practice to gently tear out the bottom of these peat pots to allow the roots greater freedom, so the plant becomes more quickly established in its outdoor location.

Preplanters If you don't want to fuss with potting soil and filling pots, then you may want to buy preplanters. These are sold under different brand names, such as Seed 'n Start and Punch 'n Grow, and can be found at garden centers. They are simply compartmented seed trays already filled with potting soil, with seeds sown into the upper soil surface. All that's required is that you place the unit in a sunny indoor location and add water. This is not the most economical way to grow a lot of annuals, since you are paying for a lot of convenience and very little seed.

Seed Tapes are another example of a product that is very convenient, but grows little seed in comparison to a traditional seed packet. The seed is prespaced along a biodegradable tape. As soon as the tape is covered over and moistened it decomposes, giving the seeds freedom to germinate at uniform distances. This system is fine if you want to grow all your flowers in straight lines—as in a cutting garden—but if you prefer to grow them in clumps or drifts of color, there isn't much benefit in using seed tape.

Plastic Pots, like peat pots, can be round or square, with the square pots generally taking up less room than the round pots. If the pots are not connected, they fit comfortably into a square seed flat. Plastic pots can be obtained in groups of six, often referred to as a "six-pack." It is quite an easy matter to detach the pots one at a time by turning them over and, by tapping sharply, the root ball will slip out for easy transplanting. Plastic pots are inexpensive, especially when bought in quantity, and they are an economical way to grow large numbers of annuals.

Plastic and Peat Seed Trays When you are fussing with starting fine seeds such as petunias and begonias, plastic and peat seed trays are the preferred choice. You simply fill them with potting soil, sow the seeds thinly over the surface, and then transfer the strongest plants into individual pots as soon as they are large enough to handle (you will be able to pull

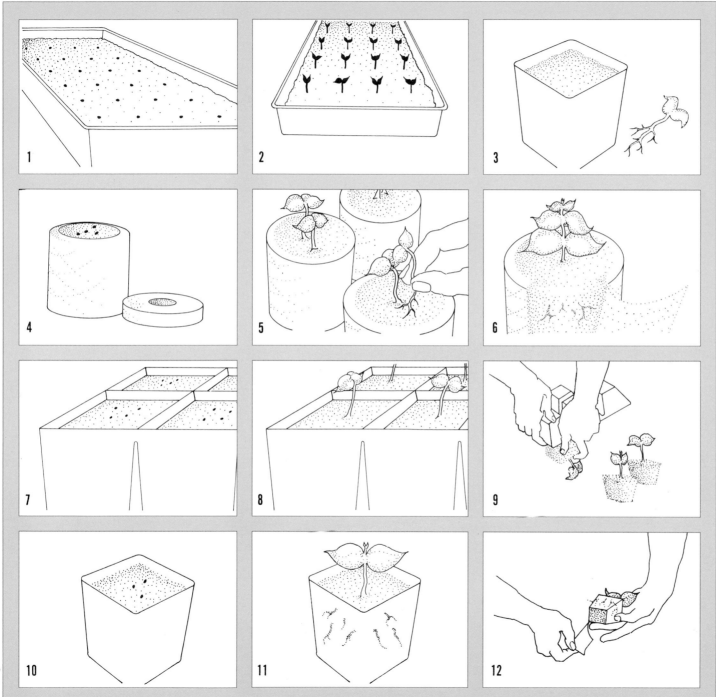

SEED-STARTING METHOD #2

7-Place seeds in individual compartments of a plastic six-pack.

8-Thin seedlings to one per compartment.

9-Press bottom of flexible plastic compartment to pop out each root ball for transplanting.

SEED-STARTING METHOD #3

10-Place seeds in fiber or peat pot.

11-Thin to one plant per pot. Let roots penetrate sides.

12-Tear out bottom of pot prior to planting.

A. M. Georgens

SMALL SEEDS—STARTING METHOD #1

1—Pour seeds into teaspoon directly from packet.

2—Pick up seeds individually with the end of moist pencil.

3—Place seeds in rows on moist paper towel.

4—Roll towel loosely. Keep warm and moist. Most fine seeds need light to germinate.

5—Examine towel after required germination period.

6—Use end of moist pencil and forefinger to pick seedlings off towel. Transfer to individual peat pots.

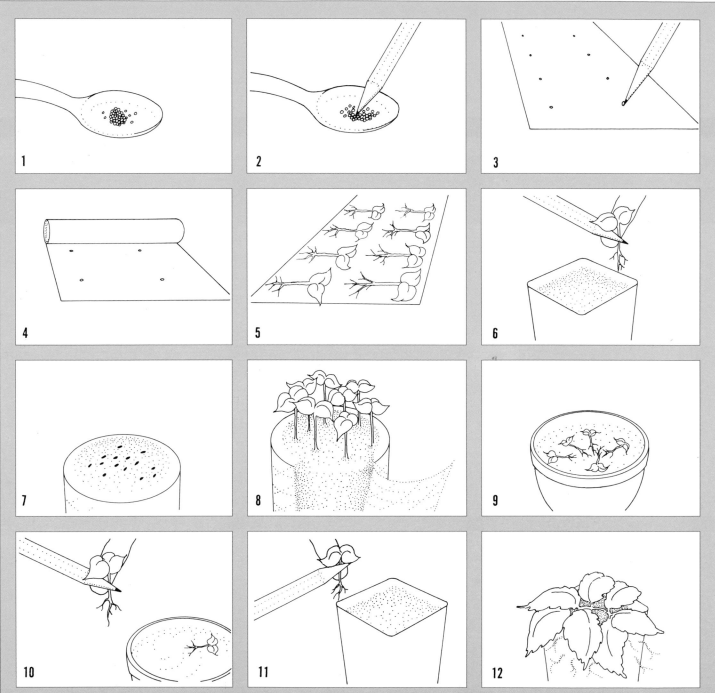

A. M. Georgens

them up using a pencil and forefinger). Avoid watering with a strong flow of water, such as from a watering can, because this will disturb the soil surface and hamper germination. It is better to keep the soil moist with a "mister" or a bottle that applies droplets of water.

Direct-Seeding of certain fast-growing flowering annuals is an easy system. Marigolds (*tagetes*), zinnias, calendula, alyssum, and celosia are examples of annuals which can be sown directly onto bare soil, lightly covered, and left to germinate without any need for starting indoors. The hardy varieties, such as calendula, can be sown several weeks before the last frost date in your area, and tender varieties, such as zinnias and marigolds can be sown after the last frost date. Before sowing the seed outdoors, take a stick or handful of flour and mark out the area designated for each different type of seed. Then take the seeds from your seed packet and scatter them so they fill the space. In the absence of natural rainfall, set a lawn sprinkler in position so that the area gets a good drink of water. Water anytime the soil looks dry, until the seedlings are up and well established.

BUYING QUALITY TRANSPLANTS

Ready-grown transplants from bedding plant outlets, such as garden centers, are a strong temptation for many good reasons, primarily the time, effort, and expense saved from fussing with seeds. However, the selection offered by these outlets is a fraction of what you might expect to find in a good mail-order seed catalog, and you will probably not be able to find anything rare or unusual. But, buying bedding plants is the closest you can come to instant color in your garden. In fact, the majority of varieties offered are likely to have at least a few flowers, so you will be able to make accurate color selections and judge the shape and size of the blooms.

Actually, the best transplants to buy are those that are not yet in bloom. Buy green and the resulting plant in your garden is likely to overcome transplant shock more easily, put on a growth spurt that catches up with the flowering transplants, and produce a greater density of color over a longer period of time.

Also, look for stocky plants rather than those that are long and lanky. When a plant is under stress—either from infrequent watering, poor light, or disease—it will often become stretched, and when transplanted to the garden may droop from transplant shock and take a long time to recover.

The best transplants are generally compact and stocky, with a dark green leaf color. Examine the leaf undersides for any signs of pest colonies such as aphids or mealybugs. Feel the potting soil and determine if it is moist or bone dry: Plants in bone dry soil may already have suffered root damage.

After you load up your car with bedding plants, go straight home and transplant your purchases as soon as possible. Do not go to the grocery store and shop, leaving the plants in a hot car where they can wilt and burn quickly once the car starts to overheat.

If any of the plants you purchase have a lead shoot that is doing all of the growing, pinch it back after you transplant so that the plant is encouraged to branch sideways and grow bushier. After transplanting, water all your plants. Be careful that tender varieties are transplanted after all danger of frost is over. If frost threatens, consider covering them with floating row covers—inexpensive, lightweight, see-through covers that rest on top of the plants and offer protection against unexpected light frost.

SOIL PREPARATION FOR ANNUALS

The most important requirement for a successful garden of annuals is proper soil preparation. Although many annuals are native to desert regions and can survive in impoverished soils, the best displays are produced by ensuring that the soil is reasonably fertile and well drained. The soil texture should be crumbly and allow freedom of root movement to a depth of at least twelve inches. Clay loam or sandy loam are both good for growing annuals, but in soil that contains a large amount of clay, adding organic matter will improve its texture. Similarly, if soil is too sandy—allowing moisture and plant nutrients to drain away too quickly—then adding liberal amounts of organic matter is essential. The best kind of organic matter is garden compost, but bales of peat, leaf

SMALL SEEDS-STARTING METHOD #2

7-Sprinkle seeds on surface of peat pellet so surface is covered. Press seeds into surface light, but do not cover. Keep moist and warm.

8-When seeds have all sprouted, tear away the pellet netting.

9-Submerge pellet in bowl of water. Soil and seedlings will separate. Seedlings will float.

10-Using moist pencil point and forefinger, gently lift seedlings individually.

11-Transfer to individual peat pots filled with planting mix.

12-When plants reach transplanting size, peat pot can be planted directly into the garden to allow freedom for roots.

Left: Red scarlet sage, blue salvia, and orange and yellow cosmos create a striking color combination in this garden.

mold, and well decomposed animal manure are also suitable.

Soil Test

A soil test will help you determine the nature of your soil. Your county cooperative extension office can test soil for you to determine its pH and the nutrients you should add. Mix the needed organic matter into the soil by digging it over and raking in the organic ingredients. If the soil needs lime (in highly acidic soils) or sulphur (in highly alkaline soils), you can add them when you are working in the organic material.

SITE SELECTION, IRRIGATION, AND AFTER CARE

Once the soil has been improved so that it is loose and fertile, and has a pH content as close to neutral as possible, you must keep it in good condition by applying compost. If the soil is not in good condition the following suggestions may help: modify the light, provide sufficient moisture, booster the applications of fertilizer, control pests and diseases, and weed the soil.

Site selection greatly depends on light, since an open meadow will produce more light than a wooded lot. However, even the removal of a single tree limb on a shaded site can be sufficient to turn a shady spot into a sunny one.

Irrigation and water retention can also make a big difference in the performance of plants that like cool conditions. If the soil is kept cool by a high humus content and watered regularly to keep it moist, shade-loving annuals, such as impatiens, coleus, and begonias, will grow in a sunny location.

Sun or Shade

Most flowering annuals prefer full sun, although there are some shade-loving varieties, such as impatiens and coleus (check list on page 127). Annuals can also be divided into cool-season annuals and warm-season annuals. Generally speaking, cool-season annuals, such as antirrhinum and calendula, are hardy and flower best during spring and early summer when the nights are still cool, or in coastal areas and high elevations where summers are mild. Conversely, warm-season annuals, such as impatiens and zinnias, are generally tender, and are damaged by frost. They grow best when the soil temperature rises and the hours of sunlight are extended. Check the individual variety descriptions, starting on page 27 to determine whether a variety is tender or hardy, warm-season or cool-season.

Irrigation

Regular amounts of water are especially important in the early stages of growth as transplants are struggling to become established. Most flowering annuals should not be watered by overhead sprinklers, since this encourages mildew and other fungal diseases; but, in the event of a drought it is better than nothing. Drip irrigation, whereby soaker hoses lay along the soil surface, covered over with a protective mulch, is the best way to irrigate flowering annuals in the absence of natural rainfall.

After Care

Fertilizer Flowering annuals are not heavy feeders in comparison to vegetables and flowering perennials. A granular, general purpose fertilizer—such as 10-10-10—raked into the upper soil surface at the start of the season, is generally sufficient to provide all the nourishment annuals need to maintain continuous bloom. (The numbers on a package of fertilizer tell you the percentages of each major plant nutrient. In this case, the fertilizer is composed of 10 percent nitrogen, 10 percent phosphorus, and 10 percent potassium. The rest is "filler," which serves as a distributing agent.) In addition to granular fertilizers, liquid fertilizers applied to the soil surface work just as well. Care should be taken that beds and borders are not overloaded with nitrogen, since this can stimulate excessive foliage growth at the expense of flowers. Nasturtiums and marigolds, for example, are particularly susceptible to excessive nitrogen.

Compost is a wonderful product to add to flower beds or borders. Well made compost not only acts as a soil conditioner so the soil is always loose and crumbly, but it also acts as a natural fertilizer. Start a compost pile in a corner of your garden simply by piling garden and kitchen waste into a heap. The best compost is made from a balance of fresh green material (such as grass clippings, leafy green hedge trimmings, potato peels, and freshly pulled weeds) plus "dead" material (such as wood ashes, sawdust, dried leaves, animal manure, and bone meal). The fresh green material provides mostly nitrogen, while the dead material produces phosphorus (especially bone meal) and potassium (especially wood ashes). Compost made from a balance of organic wastes also provides desirable trace elements, such as calcium, and when well decomposed has a pH close to neutral. Add compost to your soil twice a year if possible—in spring before transplanting, and again in autumn after the beds are cleared.

Diseases It is impossible to protect annuals from every potential disease problem. However, in areas of the country where mildew and botrytis can be problematic, consider a general purpose fungicide, such as Benlate or Benomyl. Spraying every three to four weeks can make a tremendous difference in the health and vitality of your plants—especially zinnias and geraniums which are quite vulnerable to fungus attacks. Be careful when choosing sprays, as many are hazardous to the environment. Many fungicides, however, are "organic" and after they lose their effectiveness decompose without leaving toxic substances in the atmosphere or the soil. Certain insect sprays are also "organic" (such as sprays made from rotenone, pyrethrum, or a combination of the two), and break down into harmless compost a short time after application. However, it is important to read the label of even "organic" controls to determine whether they must be kept away from children, pets, or fish, and how to dispose of unused portions.

Pests Probably the two most troublesome pests are slugs, which attack transplants during periods of wet weather, and deer (or other foraging animals), which feast on a flower bed as nonchalantly as if it were a field of corn. Slugs are best brought under control by using slug bait, available from garden centers.

Deer—and other hungry animals—are best kept out of flower beds by spraying them with a product such as Ropel, which makes the plants distasteful. Ropel must not be used on edible plants, but for ornamentals it is really the only effective deer control short of building a high fence around your property. The spray acts as a systemic, making all parts of the plant unpalatable, yet it has no odor. It remains effective up to three months.

Weeding Beds and borders for flowering annuals must be kept clear of weeds, otherwise the weeds will take over. The most effective method of weed control is a mulch applied to the soil surface after transplants are set into position; this way the annuals can grow but the weeds are suffocated. Organic mulches, such as shredded bark, cocoa-bean hulls, and shredded leaves, are both decorative and effective, though they may need topping-up as wind and weather wears the layer thin. A durable alternative is a mulch blanket that rests on top of the soil and is colored brown to look like soil. Mulch blankets are anchored at the edges with soil, and annuals are planted through it by cutting holes with scissors. Black plastic is popular as a mulch blanket because it is inexpensive; to hide its ugly appearance a thin layer of organic mulch can be spread over the top of it.

GROWING ANNUALS IN CONTAINERS

No flowering plants thrive better in containers than flowering annuals. In comparison to flowering perennials, flowering bulbs, vegetables, and small shrubs, annuals require less room for roots and they bloom for far longer periods. Even people who have plenty of room for an in-ground garden use containers because they can decorate concrete patios and wood decks, bringing color much closer to the house. Windows too can be filled with color by using window boxes and hanging baskets.

Generally speaking, the bigger the container the easier it is to grow annuals. Small containers have a tendency to dry out too quickly, so choose units with adequate space and soil depth. Generally speaking, anything less than a one gallon capacity will need watering daily. Garden centers offer a wide

Right, above: Impatiens decorate circular wooden planters on this deck.
Right, below: A container planted with purple cineraria, a popular annual to grow under glass.
Opposite page: Dahlberg Daisy (*Dyssodia tenuifolia*) has become a popular annual for containers.

choice of containers, but it's a lot more fun to rummage through flea markets and secondhand stores for some offbeat containers, such as rusty old cauldrons and horse troughs. Select containers with drainage holes in them, since the roots will rot if water doesn't drain freely. If drainage holes don't exist—and you cannot bore them into the container yourself—then consider a layer of crushed stones and charcoal in the bottom as a "drainage field," taking care that you don't apply more water than the drainage area can hold.

Select only containers made of problem-free materials. For example, unless they are situated in a shaded area, plastic and steel can overheat and burn delicate root hairs on hot, sunny days. Better alternatives to these two are clay, ceramic, or wood, since all of these materials tend to keep the soil cool.

The best soil for containers is a blend of a commercial peat-based potting soil, such as Pro-Mix, with some good garden loam. This combination provides good anchorage and moisture holding capacity. If you are using wooden containers—such as whiskey half barrels—consider lining the inside with a plastic garbage bag so the soil is kept clear of the wood to resist rotting.

Unless hanging baskets are in a cool, shady area plastic is not as good as a wire basket that has moist sphagnum moss lining the edges. Hanging baskets are especially prone to overheating and drying out, because of the free air circulation around them, but the moist sphagnum helps prevent rapid evaporation. Also, plants can be pushed through the sides of the basket to give a rounded, well filled look compared to a plastic basket that can only be planted around the upper rim.

Although just about every kind of annual can be grown in some kind of container, plant breeders have developed special kinds of annuals to look extremely attractive in both pots and hanging baskets. When considering annuals for containers, pay particular attention to those described as "cascading," for example cascading lobelia and cascading petunias. Instead of growing up, they tend to grow sideways and spill down over the edges of a pot or hanging basket so that the container can be completely hidden with foliage or flowers.

Beds & Borders Annuals can be displayed at their best in beds and borders. Generally, a bed is any plot of soil surrounded on all sides by paving or lawn, and is capable of

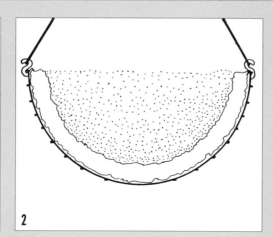

A. M. Georgens

Opposite page: The 'Futura' variety of impatiens makes a beautiful, colorful hanging basket in a partially shaded location.

Left: Three stages of preparing a hanging basket: (1) place wire basket over a bucket to keep it stable while filling; (2) line inside of wire basket with moist sphagnum moss like a nest, then fill the nest with potting soil; (3) the finished basket is shown here planted with an assortment of annuals.

being viewed from many directions. Beds can be round, square, rectangular, oval, or kidney-shaped. A border usually backs up to something vertical—such as a hedge, fence, or wall—and it is most often viewed from one direction, or from an angle.

To facilitate drainage, beds are often mounded in the middle, and for best display the tallest plants are also situated in the middle. In a bed, the shortest plants—called "edging" plants—are placed around the perimeter. With borders the soil is usually highest in back, and that is where the tallest plants are placed. Edging plants are placed at the front of the border, with medium-height plants sandwiched between the tall background plants and low edging plants.

Annuals are frequently mixed with perennials in perennial borders, rock gardens, and water gardens in order to maintain color throughout the season as the perennials come in and out of bloom. For example, in a perennial border alyssum, ageratum, and dwarf begonias are popular to use for edging, while cleome, sunflowers (*Helianthus annuus*), and snapdragons (*Antirrhinum majus*) are popular for tall highlights. Cosmos, salvia farinacea, and American marigolds (*Tagetes erecta*) are examples of medium-height annuals that combine well with perennials.

In rock gardens, low-growing plants like verbena, alyssum, dahlberg daisy (*Dyssodia tenuilobia*), and nasturtiums can turn an average planting of perennials into something vibrant and special.

For making water gardens more colorful—especially the margins of ponds and streambanks—try some of the new mixtures of mimulus (monkey flowers), along with impatiens, coleus, begonias, and browallia.

Cutting Garden Many people like to grow annuals solely for the sake of cutting them to make lovely indoor flower arrangements, but dislike taking them from beds and borders. It makes sense, therefore, to set aside a special area to grow plants specially for cutting. Usually, this area is located near the vegetable garden so that flowers for the house and edibles for the kitchen can be gathered together.

A good layout for cutting gardens is the "straight-row" system often used in vegetable gardens. Annuals can be grown in fifteen foot rows (or longer), with walkways between each row to make gathering the flowers easy. The best cutting gardens have a balance between long-stemmed flowers suitable for fresh arrangements—such as marigolds (*Tagetes*), zinnias, and snapdragons (*Antirrhinum*)—and "everlastings,"—such as strawflowers (*Helichrysum*), immortelle (*Xeranthemum*), and globe amaranth (*Gomphrena*)—which are easily dried to make dried flower arrangements.

Right: An easy way to water a flower garden is to leave a lawn sprinkler in place and turn it on whenever your garden needs watering. To be most effective, you should give your garden a thorough soaking, making sure that the water reaches the roots of your plants.

Opposite page:
The research farm of the flower breeders, Goldsmith Seeds, near Gilroy, California, is a sea of color in summer from trial plantings of petunias, portulacea, and other vibrant annuals.

CHAPTER TWO

THE ENCYCLOPEDIA OF ESSENTIAL ANNUALS

THE FOLLOWING 100 SUPERLATIVE ANNUALS for garden display have been chosen mostly for their ornamental value.

They are listed alphabetically by their botanical (Latin) name because this most consistently identifies garden annuals better than their common names. While many annuals have popular common names—'French Marigold' for *Tagetes patula*—others do not have such familiar common names or else are widely known by two or more common names—*Impatiens wallerana*, for example is often called plain 'Impatiens,' 'Busy Lizzies,' or 'Patience Plant.'

To find a description for any annual where you know only the common name, simply turn to the index for a quick cross-reference.

The heights given are mostly mature heights when the plants start to flower. Often, with good soil or prolonged rainfall, or late in the season, plants may exceed the heights stated here.

BOTANICAL NAME *Ageratum houstonianum*

COMMON NAME Floss Flower

RANGE Native to Central America. Tender annual.

HEIGHT 12 inches; mounded habit.

CULTURE Easy to grow in well-drained, garden loam soil, in full sun. Start seeds indoors at 70° to 75°F and set 8-week-old transplants, spaced 8 inches apart, into the soil after all danger of frost.

DESCRIPTION Fluffy mauve pink, blue, or white flower clusters bloom all summer on compact plants. Leaves are broad, oval, pointed, dark green. Excellent for edging beds and borders.

RECOMMENDED VARIETY Blue Danube, a lovely blue hybrid variety.

BOTANICAL NAME *Alcea rosea*

COMMON NAME Hollyhock

RANGE Native to China. Hardy annual.

HEIGHT Up to 10 feet; erect, spirelike habit.

CULTURE Easy to grow in any well-drained, garden loam soil in full sun. Start seeds indoors at 70° to 75°F and set 6-week-old transplants, spaced 12 inches apart, into the soil after danger of heavy frost. Can be seeded directly into the soil, but may not bloom until following year in short-season areas.

DESCRIPTION Single- and double-flowered kinds are available, clustered along strong stems, forming beautiful flower spikes. Color range includes pink, red, white, and yellow. Leaves are large, heart shaped, dark green. Good for tall backgrounds and as an accent against walls, fences, and buildings.

RECOMMENDED VARIETY 'Summer Carnival' (extra large pomponlike flowers). A dwarf variety, 'Majorette' (2 feet), can be used for bedding.

BOTANICAL NAME *Amaranthus tricolor*

COMMON NAME Joseph's-coat

RANGE Native to Mexico. Tender annual.

HEIGHT 3 to 4 feet; erect habit.

CULTURE Easy to grow in any well-drained, garden loam soil in full sun. Start seed indoors at 70° to 75°F and set 6-week-old-transplants, spaced 12 inches apart, into the garden after all danger of frost.

DESCRIPTION The top most leaves, colored red, orange, green, and yellow, arch out like a fountain. A popular accent for mixed beds and borders.

RECOMMENDED VARIETY 'Illumination' old leaves are chocolate colored; new leaves are brilliant orange-red.

BOTANICAL NAME *Anchusa capensis*

COMMON NAME Summer Forget-me-not

RANGE Native to South America. Biennial grown as hardy annual.

HEIGHT 12 inches; low, mounded habit.

CULTURE Easy to grow in any well-drained loam soil in full sun. Start seed at 60°F and set out 6- to 8-week-old transplants, spaced 6 to 12 inches apart, several weeks before the last frost date. Flowers best when nights are cool.

DESCRIPTION Blue flowers are clustered on branching stems. Leaves are bright green, lancelike. Good to use for edging beds and borders.

BOTANICAL NAME *Antirrhinum majus*

COMMON NAME Snapdragon

RANGE Native to the Mediterranean. Hardy annual.

HEIGHT Up to 3 feet; erect, spirelike habit.

CULTURE Start seed indoors at 70° to 75°F and set 8-week-old transplants, spaced 12 inches apart, into the garden after danger of heavy frosts.

DESCRIPTION Tubular flowers are arranged in spikes, some with closed mouths, others with open throats. Colors include red, yellow, orange, pink, white, and bicolors. Leaves are narrow, lancelike, dark green. Excellent for mass plantings in beds and borders. Tall kinds, such as the 'Rockets' are good for cutting. Dwarf kinds, such as 'Floral Carpet' are excellent for edging and low beds.

BOTANICAL NAME *Arctotis stoechadifolia*

COMMON NAME African Daisy

RANGE Native to South Africa. Tender annual.

HEIGHT 12 to 15 inches; clump-forming habit.

CULTURE Easy to grow in any fertile, well-drained loam soil in full sun. Prefers cool nights. Start seed indoors with the soil temperature at 60° to 70°F, and set 6- to 8-week-old transplants, spaced 12 inches apart, into the garden after all danger of frost. Also can be direct-seeded.

DESCRIPTION Daisy-like flowers are borne on slender stems in yellow, orange, red, and pink, plus bicolors. Leaves are bright green, toothed. Popular for mixed beds and borders, especially in coastal gardens. Good for cutting.

BOTANICAL NAME *Begonia semperflorens*

COMMON NAME Wax Begonia

RANGE Native to South America. Tender annual.

HEIGHT 8 to 12 inches; low, compact habit.

CULTURE Prefers moist, humus-rich, fertile loam soil in partial shade. Hybrids will tolerate full sun. Start seed indoors at 70° to 85°F soil temperature and set 10- to 12-week-old transplants, spaced 6 to 10 inches apart, into the garden after all danger of frost.

DESCRIPTION Masses of white, pink, or red flowers cover mound-shaped plants, with either bright green or bronze foliage, depending on variety. Exceptional for massing in beds and borders. Also good for containers, including hanging baskets.

RECOMMENDED VARIETY 'Cocktail' series, featuring bronze foliage.

BOTANICAL NAME *Brachycome iberidifolia*

COMMON NAME Swan River Daisy

RANGE Native to Australia. Tender annual.

HEIGHT 12 inches; bushy, mounded habit.

CULTURE Prefers a moist, fertile, humus-rich loam soil in full sun. Flowers best when nights are cool. Start seeds indoors at 60° to 70°F soil temperature and set 6-week-old transplants, spaced 12 inches apart, into the garden after all danger of frost.

DESCRIPTION Covers itself in blue or white daisy-like flowers. Leaves are small, toothed, dark green. Good for massing in mixed beds and borders. Popular in coastal gardens.

BOTANICAL NAME *Brassica oleracea*

COMMON NAME Ornamental Cabbage; Ornamental Kale

RANGE Developed from species native to Europe. Hardy annual.

HEIGHT 12 inches; low, mound-shaped habit.

CULTURE Easy to grow in any well-drained, fertile loam soil in full sun. Does best when nights are cool. Start seeds indoors at 65° to 85°F soil temperature and plant 6- to 8-week-old transplants, spaced 12 inches apart, in the garden several weeks before the last expected frost date.

DESCRIPTION Mostly white or pink frilly leaves form a decorative rosette at the center of cabbagelike plants; all other leaves are blue-green. Popular for edging beds and borders and for massing. Good for fall color since the plants like cool temperatures and withstand heavy frosts.

BOTANICAL NAME *Browallia speciosa*

COMMON NAME Lovely Browallia

RANGE Native to South America. Tender annual.

HEIGHT 12 inches; mounded, bushy habit.

CULTURE Prefers a moist, fertile, humus-rich soil in partial shade. Start seed indoors at 70° to 85°F soil temperature and set 8- to 10-week-old transplants, spaced 12 inches apart, into the garden after all danger of frost.

DESCRIPTION Masses of blue or white flowers resembling small petunias cover the plants all summer. Leaves are lancelike, delicate, bright green. Suitable for massing in shady beds and borders. Popular for containers, especially hanging baskets.

RECOMMENDED VARIETY 'Blue Bells Improved.'

BOTANICAL NAME *Calendula officinalis*

COMMON NAME Pot-marigold

RANGE Native to the Mediterranean. Hardy annual.

HEIGHT 12 inches; bushy habit.

CULTURE Easy to grow in any well-drained loam soil in full sun. Does best when nights are cool. Start seeds indoors at 70°F soil temperature and set 6-week-old transplants, spaced 12 inches apart, into the garden several weeks before the last expected frost. Also can be direct-seeded.

DESCRIPTION Mostly yellow and orange double flowers held erect on stiff stems. Leaves are dark green, indented, have a spicy odor. Suitable for mixed beds and borders.

RECOMMENDED VARIETY: 'Pacific Beauty.'

BOTANICAL NAME *Callistephus chinensis*

COMMON NAME China Aster

RANGE Native to China. Tender annual.

HEIGHT 1 to 3 feet; upright, branching habit.

CULTURE Easy to grow in any fertile, well-drained loam soil in full sun. Start seed indoors at 60° to 70°F soil temperature and set out 6-week-old transplants, spaced 12 inches apart, after all danger of frost. Flowers best when nights are cool.

DESCRIPTION Double- and semi-double chrysanthemum-like flowers are mostly red, pink, white, and blue. Leaves are dark green, serrated. Popular as an accent in beds and borders. Dwarf types, such as 'Dwarf Queen' are suitable for edging. Tall kinds, such as 'Giant Perfection' are excellent for cutting.

BOTANICAL NAME *Capsicum annuum*

COMMON NAME Ornamental Pepper

RANGE Native to South America. Tender annual.

HEIGHT 10 inches; compact, bushy habit.

CULTURE Prefers fertile, well-drained, sandy loam soil in full sun. Start seeds indoors at 70° to 85°F soil temperature and set 8 to 10 week-old transplants into the garden, spaced 8 inches apart, after all danger of frost.

DESCRIPTION Low, mounded plants cover themselves with round or cone-shaped fruits that ripen from green to orange and red. Excellent for edging beds and borders, also for growing in containers.

RECOMMENDED VARIETY 'Holiday Cheer' bears round, marble-size fruit.

BOTANICAL NAME *Catharanthus roseus*

COMMON NAME Vinca; Periwinkle

RANGE Native to Madagascar. Tender annual.

HEIGHT 12 inches; low, spreading habit.

CULTURE Easy to grow in any well-drained, fertile loam soil in full sun or partial shade. Drought tolerant. Start seeds indoors at 70° to 85°F and set 10-week-old transplants into the garden, spaced 12 inches apart, after all danger of frost.

DESCRIPTION Star-shaped flowers are flowering continuously. Blossoms are mostly white, pink, or purple with contrasting red centers on plants that freely branch sideways. Glossy, dark green, broad, pointed leaves look like evergreen needles. Popular for edging beds and borders, also as a ground cover and for cascading from window boxes.

RECOMMENDED VARIETY 'Little Linda' is a prolific, flowering purple.

This sensible planting scheme features tall cosmos as a background, blue salvia in the middle, and dwarf French marigolds in the foreground.

BOTANICAL NAME *Celosia cristata*

COMMON NAME Crested Cockscomb

RANGE Native to Asia. Tender annual.

HEIGHT Up to 3 feet; erect, bushy habit.

CULTURE Easy to grow in any fertile, well-drained loam soil in full sun. Start seeds indoors at 70° to 85°F soil temperature and set 5-week-old transplants into the garden, spaced 12 inches apart, after all danger of frost. Older transplants tend to suffer shock. Also can be direct-seeded.

DESCRIPTION The flowers of crested cockscomb resemble lumps of brain coral held erect above long, spear-shaped, green leaves. Good for massing in beds and borders. Excellent for cutting and drying for arrangements.

RECOMMENDED VARIETY 'Floradale' bears large globular heads on compact plants.

RELATED SPECIES *C. plumosa* bears flowers that resemble feathery plumes.

BOTANICAL NAME *Centaurea cyanus*

COMMON NAME Bachelor's-button; Cornflower

RANGE Native to Europe. Hardy annual.

HEIGHT 3 feet; erect habit.

CULTURE Easy to grow in any well-drained loam soil in full sun. Start seed indoors at 70°F soil temperature and set 4-week-old transplants into the garden. Older transplants tend to wilt. Also can be direct-seeded.

DESCRIPTION Mostly blue, white, pink, or red flowers are held erect on slender stems. Leaves are dark green, lancelike. Popular for mixed beds and borders, also for wildflower meadow gardens. Excellent for cutting.

RECOMMENDED VARIETY 'Blue Diadem' bears large blue flowers.

BOTANICAL NAME *Chrysanthemum carinatum*

COMMON NAME Painted Daisy

RANGE Native to Morocco. Hardy annual.

HEIGHT 3 feet; erect, bushy habit.

CULTURE Easy to grow in any well-drained, fertile loam soil in full sun. Start seed indoors at 60° to 70°F soil temperature and set 6-week-old transplants into the garden, spaced 12 inches apart, 3 weeks before the last expected frost date. Also can be direct-seeded.

DESCRIPTION Daisy-like flowers are ringed with several bands of contrasting colors, mostly in variations of red, white, and yellow. Leaves are dark green, toothed. Good for mixed beds and borders. Often included in wildflower meadow mixtures. Excellent for cutting.

RECOMMENDED VARIETY 'Rainbow Mixed Colors.'

BOTANICAL NAME *Clarkia amoena*

COMMON NAME Godetia; Satin Flower

RANGE Native to California. Hardy annual.

HEIGHT 12 inches; bushy, clump-forming habit.

CULTURE Easy to grow in any well-drained loam soil in full sun. Thrives best when direct-seeded. If desired, start seed indoors at 60°F soil temperature and set out 6-week-old transplants, spaced 12 inches apart, several weeks before the last frost date. Older plants suffer transplant shock. Flowers best when nights are cool.

DESCRIPTION Lovely, cup-shaped flowers with crinkled petals and a satinlike sheen cover the plants in early summer. Colors include white, pink, red, purple, and bicolors. Leaves are narrow, pointed, dark green. Popular in coastal gardens for beds and borders.

RECOMMENDED VARIETY 'Dwarf Mixed Colors.'

BOTANICAL NAME *Cleome hasslerana*

COMMON NAME Spiderflower

RANGE Native to Central America. Tender annual.

HEIGHT Up to 5 feet; tall, spirelike habit.

CULTURE Easy to grow in any well-drained loam soil in full sun. Start seed indoors at 70° to 85°F soil temperature and set out 6-week-old transplants, spaced 12 inches apart, after all danger of frost.

DESCRIPTION Ball-shaped flower heads have a spidery appearance from long, slender filaments that support the flowers, and pointed seed pods that project beyond the flowers. Color range includes pink, white, and purple. Leaves are deeply indented, dark green. Popular as a background in beds and borders. Also suitable for cutting.

BOTANICAL NAME *Cobaea scandens*

COMMON NAME Cup-and-saucer vine

RANGE Native to Central America. Tender annual.

HEIGHT Up to 10 feet; vining habit.

CULTURE Easy to grow in any fertile, well-drained loam soil in full sun. Start seeds indoors at 70° to 85°F soil temperature and set out 6- to 8-week-old transplants, spaced 3 feet apart, after all danger of frost. Needs support to climb.

DESCRIPTION Unusual flowers resemble Canterbury Bells, and are pollinated by bats in their native lands. Colors include violet-blue, purple, and white-tinted pink or green. Mostly used to cover chain-link fences or train on a trellis or wall.

BOTANICAL NAME *Coleus* x *hybrida*

COMMON NAME Flame Nettle

RANGE Native to Indonesia. Tender annual.

HEIGHT 2 feet; bushy habit.

CULTURE Prefers fertile, humus-rich, moist loam soil in partial shade. Start seed indoors at 70° to 85°F soil temperature and set out 8- to 10-week-old transplants, spaced 12 inches apart, after all danger of frost, in partial shade.

DESCRIPTION Grown mostly for the vibrant color of its leaves, sometimes three contrasting colors appear together, with no two leaves exactly alike. Colors include yellow, red, orange, lime green, dark green, and mahogany. The decorative appearance of the leaves is often enhanced by scalloped or ruffled margins. Popular for beds and borders, also containers, including hanging baskets.

BOTANICAL NAME *Consolida ambigua*

COMMON NAME Larkspur

RANGE Native to Southern Europe. Hardy annual.

HEIGHT 3 feet; upright, spirelike habit.

CULTURE Easy to grow in any fertile, well-drained loam soil in full sun. Start seed indoors at 60° to 70°F and set out 6- to 8-week-old transplants, spaced 12 inches apart, after danger of frost. Also can be direct-seeded. May need staking.

DESCRIPTION Beautiful flower spikes resemble small delphinium. Color range includes white, blue, purple, and pink. Leaves are fern-like. Good as tall backgrounds for beds and borders. Excellent for cutting, and for dried flower arrangements.

BOTANICAL NAME *Coreopsis tinctoria*

COMMON NAME Calliopsis

RANGE Native to North America. Hardy annual.

HEIGHT 1 to 2 feet; bushy habit.

CULTURE Easy to grow in any fertile, well-drained loam soil in full sun. Start seed indoors at 70°F soil temperature and set out 6-week-old transplants, spaced 12 inches apart, after all danger of frost.

DESCRIPTION Produces an abundance of daisy-like flowers on airy plants with fine, green leaves. Colors include yellow, orange, red, and mahogany, plus bicolors. Good for beds and borders, also for wildflower meadows. Tall kinds suitable for cutting.

RECOMMENDED VARIETY 'Dwarf Mixed Colors' grow compact, mound plants (6 to 8 inches) suitable for edging.

BOTANICAL NAME *Cosmos bipinnatus*

COMMON NAME Cosmos

RANGE Native to Mexico. Tender annual.

HEIGHT 3 to 5 feet; upright, branching habit.

CULTURE Easy to grow in any fertile, well-drained loam soil in full sun. Start seed indoors at 70° to 85°F soil temperature and set out 6-week-old transplants, spaced 12 inches apart, after all danger of frost. Also can be direct-seeded.

DESCRIPTION Flowers resemble single-flowered Dahlias on airy plants with fine, feathery leaves. Color range includes red, white, pink, and bicolors. Good for tall backgrounds in beds and borders, also for wildflower meadows. Excellent for cutting.

RECOMMENDED VARIETY 'Sensation' mixed colors.

RELATED SPECIES *C. sulphurues*, including 'Diablo' with deep orange flowers and 'Sunny Gold,' a dwarf yellow just 12 inches high.

BOTANICAL NAME *Cucurbita pepo*

COMMON NAME Ornamental Gourds

RANGE Native to South America. Tender annual.

HEIGHT 10 feet; vining habit.

CULTURE Easy to grow in any well-drained loam soil in full sun. Start seed at 70° to 85°F and set out 4-week-old transplants, spaced at least 3 feet apart, after danger of frost.

DESCRIPTION Vigorous vines with heart-shaped leaves are grown mostly for the decorative fruit, which vary not only in shape but also in their color combinations. Some fruit are shaped like apples, pears, and oranges with beige, yellow, orange, and green coloring. Flowers are yellow, inconspicuous. Good for covering trellises and fences. A similar gourd species *Lagenaria siceria* ('Bottle Gourds') are popular for making bird houses and dippers.

BOTANICAL NAME *Cynoglossum amabile*

COMMON NAME Chinese Forget-me-not

RANGE Native to China. Hardy annual.

HEIGHT 2 feet; clump-forming habit.

CULTURE Easy to grow in any fertile, well-drained loam soil. Start seed at 70° to 85°F and set out 8-week-old transplants, spaced 12 inches apart, several weeks before the last expected frost date.

DESCRIPTION Dainty, star-shaped flowers resemble forget-me-nots, vary in color from deep blue to pale blue to white. Good accent for mixed beds and borders. Suitable for cutting.

This colorful annual border in midsummer features red scarlet sage, blue ageratum, yellow marigolds, and pink spider flowers.

BOTANICAL NAME *Dahlia* x *hybrida*

COMMON NAME Bedding Dahlias

RANGE Native to Mexico. Tender annual.

HEIGHT 1 to 3 feet; upright, bushy habit.

CULTURE Prefers a moist, fertile, humus-rich loam soil in full sun. Start seeds indoors at 60°F soil temperature and set out 8-week-old transplants, spaced 12 inches apart, after all danger of frost.

DESCRIPTION Single or double flowers have mostly rounded petals. Color range includes yellow, white, orange, pink, red, and mahogany. Leaves can be bright green or bronze in color. Good for massing in beds and borders. Excellent for cutting.

RECOMMENDED VARIETY 'Rigoletto,' with a dwarf, compact habit and wide color range. Not to be confused with tuberous dahlias which are taller and capable of growing flowers the size of dinner plates.

BOTANICAL NAME *Datura metel*

COMMON NAME Angel's Trumpet

RANGE Native to South America. Tender annual.

HEIGHT 2 to 3 feet; mounded, sprawling habit.

CULTURE Easy to grow in any well-drained loam or sandy soil in full sun. Start seed at 70° to 85°F and set out 6-week-old transplants, spaced at least 2 feet apart, after all danger of frost.

DESCRIPTION White trumpet-shaped flowers up to 6 inches long are borne freely all summer. Dark green leaves are spear-shaped. Good accent for mixed beds and borders. Suitable for growing in containers. Caution: all parts are poisonous.

BOTANICAL NAME *Delphinium elatum*

COMMON NAME Delphinium

RANGE Native to Northern Europe. Biennials best treated as hardy annuals.

HEIGHT 3 to 5 feet; spirelike habit.

CULTURE Prefers a moist, fertile, humus-rich loam soil in full sun and sheltered from winds. Start seed indoors at 70° to 80°F soil temperature and set out 12-week-old transplants several weeks before the last expected frost date. Usually needs staking. Flowers best when nights are cool, and in coastal locations.

DESCRIPTION Columnlike flower spikes are studded with flat flowers that have contrasting centers called "bees," which are usually black or white. The flowers' color range includes white, blue, purple, and pink. Excellent for tall backgrounds in beds and borders. Superb cut flower.

RECOMMENDED VARIETY 'Pacific Giants' grow to a height of 6 feet. Seedsmen also offer a strain known as *Belladonna* hybrids, such as 'Connecticut Yankees,' which grow compact and bushy (2½ feet).

BOTANICAL NAME *Dianthus caryophyllus*

COMMON NAME Carnation

RANGE Native to Europe. Tender perennials best grown as tender annuals.

HEIGHT 2 feet; upright, bushy habit.

CULTURE Easy to grow in any fertile, well-drained loam soil in full sun. Start seed at 70°F soil temperature and set out 8-week-old transplants, spaced 12 inches apart, after danger of frost.

DESCRIPTION Fragrant double flowers are white, yellow, red, pink, and mahogany on slender stems. Gray-green leaves are slender, pointed. Tall kinds such as 'Chabaud Giants' are good for cutting. Dwarf varieties such as the 'Knights' are suitable for massing in beds and borders.

BOTANICAL NAME *Dianthus chinensis*

COMMON NAME Dianthus

RANGE Native to China. Hardy annual.

HEIGHT 12 inches; compact, mounded habit.

CULTURE Easy to grow in any well-drained loam soil in full sun. Start seed indoors at 70°F and set out 8-week-old transplants, spaced 6 to 12 inches apart, several weeks before the last frost date.

DESCRIPTION Fragrant flowers with frilly petal edges are borne in profusion. Color range includes red, white, and pink—sometimes with a contrasting red eye at the petal center. Gray-green leaves are narrow, pointed. Popular for massing in low beds and borders; also for edging and rock gardens. Tall kinds are good for cutting.

RECOMMENDED VARIETY 'Magic Charms,' an early, free flowering (having abundant growth spurts) plant.

BOTANICAL NAME *Digitalis purpurea*

COMMON NAME Foxglove; Foxy

RANGE Native to Europe. Biennial best treated as an annual.

HEIGHT 4 to 5 feet; erect, spirelike habit.

CULTURE Prefers a fertile, moist, well-drained loam soil in partial shade. Start seed indoors at 70°F and set out 10-week-old transplants, spaced 12 inches apart, several weeks before the last frost date. Can be direct-seeded. Most Foxgloves bloom the second year after sowing seed, but Foxy is an exception, blooming in the summer of the first year. Flowers best when nights are cool.

DESCRIPTION Spotted, tubular florets form a spectacular flower spike. Color range includes white, pink, purple, red, and yellow; the throats are handsomely spotted. Leaves are dark green, heart shaped, hairy. Popular for shady beds and borders as a tall background. Good for cutting. Caution: seeds and other parts are poisonous if eaten.

BOTANICAL NAME *Dimorphotheca sinuata*

COMMON NAME Cape Marigold; African Daisy

RANGE Native to South Africa. Tender annual.

HEIGHT 12 inches; compact, mounded habit.

CULTURE Easy to grow in any well-drained loam soil in full sun. Start seeds indoors at 60° to 70°F and set out 4-week-old transplants, spaced 12 inches apart, after all danger of frost. Also can be direct-seeded.

DESCRIPTION Daisy-like flowers have shimmering petals in white, yellow, orange, and pink with prominent black eyes. Dark green leaves are small, serrated. Good for edging low beds and borders. Especially popular for rock gardens in coastal areas.

BOTANICAL NAME *Dorotheanus bellidiformis*

COMMON NAME Livingstone Daisy

RANGE Native to South Africa. Tender annual.

HEIGHT 6 inches; low, spreading habit.

CULTURE Easy to grow in any well-drained loam or sandy soil in full sun. Start seed indoors at 60°F soil temperature and set out 8-week-old transplants, spaced 8 inches apart, after all danger of frost. Also can be direct-seeded in mild climates. Flowers best when nights are cool.

DESCRIPTION Flowers have shimmering petals, borne in such profusion that they can completely hide the foliage. Colors include purple, pink, orange, apricot, and yellow, plus bicolors. Good for edging low beds and borders.

RECOMMENDED VARIETY 'Yellow Ice,' an early flowering yellow.

BOTANICAL NAME *Dyssodia tenuiloba*

COMMON NAME Dahlberg Daisy

RANGE Native to Mexico. Tender annual.

HEIGHT 6 inches; low, spreading habit.

CULTURE Easy to grow in any well-drained, fertile loam soil in full sun. Start seed indoors at 60° to 80°F soil temperature and set out 6- to 8-week-old transplants, spaced at least 6 inches apart, after all danger of frost. Also can be direct-seeded. Drought resistant.

DESCRIPTION Dainty yellow flowers are borne in great profusion all summer on airy plants that hug the ground. Excellent for edging beds and borders. Makes a good temporary ground cover and is suitable for containers.

BOTANICAL NAME *Eschscholzia californica*

COMMON NAME California-poppy

RANGE Native to California. Hardy annual.

HEIGHT 12 inches; compact, mounded habit.

CULTURE Easy to grow in any well-drained loam soil in full sun. Start seeds indoors at 60°F soil temperature and set out 4-week-old transplants, spaces 12 inches apart, several weeks before the last frost date. Older transplants suffer shock. Can be direct-seeded. Self-seeds easily. Flowers best when nights are cool.

DESCRIPTION Poppy-like flowers have a satin sheen. Colors include yellow, orange, pink, white, and red. Leaves are narrow, pointed. Popular for massing in beds and borders, also wildflower meadows.

RECOMMENDED VARIETY 'Ballerina,' a rich mixture with crinkled petals.

BOTANICAL NAME *Euphorbia marginata*

COMMON NAME Snow-on-the-Mountain

RANGE Native to North America. Tender annual.

HEIGHT 2 to 3 feet; erect, bushy habit.

CULTURE Easy to grow in any well-drained loam soil in full sun. Tolerates drought and sandy soil. Start seed indoors at 70°F and set out 6- to 8-week-old transplants, spaced 12 inches apart, after danger of frost. Also can be direct-seeded.

DESCRIPTION The attractive silvery green foliage becomes even more ornamental when the leaf tips produce clusters of white-edged leaves with tiny white flowers clustered in the middle of each whorl. Popular as an accent in mixed beds and borders. Caution: A milky sap that seeps from the stem when cut may cause skin irritation.

BOTANICAL NAME *Gaillardia pulchella*

COMMON NAME Blanket Flower

RANGE Native to North America. Tender annual.

HEIGHT 3 feet; erect, bushy habit.

CULTURE Easy to grow in any well-drained loam soil in full sun. Start seed indoors 70° to 85°F and set out 6-week-old transplants, spaced 12 inches apart, after danger of frost. Also can be direct-seeded.

DESCRIPTION Double- and semi-double flowers are yellow, orange, and red, plus bicolors. Leaves are dark green, narrow, serrated. Good for massing in beds and borders. Popular for wildflower meadows. Suitable for cutting.

BOTANICAL NAME *Gazania rigens*

COMMON NAME Rainbow Daisy

RANGE Native to South Africa. Tender annual.

HEIGHT 12 inches; low, spreading habit.

CULTURE Easy to grow in any well-drained loam soil in full sun. Start seed indoors at 60°F soil temperature and set out 6-week-old transplants, spaced 12 inches apart, after danger of frost. Flowers close up on cloudy days.

DESCRIPTION Shimmering flowers are mostly yellow, orange, pink, red, and mahogany with black zone around the petal center. Dark green leaves are narrow, pointed. Good for mixed beds and borders.

RECOMMENDED VARIETY 'Mini Star,' a dwarf compact variety good for rock gardens and for creating a ground cover effect.

BOTANICAL NAME *Gomphrena globosa*

COMMON NAME Globe Amaranth

RANGE Native to India. Tender annual.

HEIGHT Up to 2 feet; bushy, mounded habit.

CULTURE Easy to grow in any well-drained loam soil in full sun. Start seed indoors at 70° to 85°F and set out 6-week-old transplants, spaced 12 inches apart, after danger of frost. Also can be direct-seeded. Extremely drought resistant.

DESCRIPTION Clover-like flowers are mostly white, orange, pink, and purple. Dark green leaves are spear shaped. Good for massing in beds and borders. Popular both as a fresh cut flower and for dried arrangements.

BOTANICAL NAME *Gypsophila elegans*

COMMON NAME Baby's-breath

RANGE Native to Europe. Tender annual.

HEIGHT 2 feet; bushy, cloudlike habit.

CULTURE Easy to grow in any well-drained loam soil in full sun. Start seed indoors at 70°F and set out 4- to 5-week-old transplants, spaced 12 inches apart, after all danger of frost. Also can be direct-seeded. Drought tolerant.

DESCRIPTION Dainty white or light pink aspirin-size flowers are borne in such profusion on billowing plants that they appear to be a cloud of mist when seen from a distance. Stems and leaves are delicate, wispy. Popular as an accent in mixed beds and borders. Excellent for cutting.

RECOMMENDED VARIETY: 'Covent Garden.'

BOTANICAL NAME *Helianthus annuus*

COMMON NAME Sunflower

RANGE Native to North America. Tender annual.

HEIGHT Up to 8 feet; upright habit.

CULTURE Easy to grow in any well-drained loam soil in full sun. Start seed indoors at 70° to 85°F and set out 4-week-old transplants, spaced 3 feet apart, after all danger of frost. Generally flowers just as fast from direct-seeding.

DESCRIPTION Some varieties of sunflowers have the largest flowers in the plant kingdom, with individual flower heads up to 24 inches across. Their centers are full of edible nutlike seeds, which are surrounded by golden yellow petals. Dwarf or branching varieties with smaller flowers are more popular for ornamental display, such as 'Teddy Bear,' with full double flowers resembling those in the famous Van Gogh painting, and 'Color Fashion,' a tall mixture of yellow, bronze, red, and purple single-flowered types good for cutting and backgrounds.

An effective companion planting of perennial orange gloriosa daisies and annual phlox.

BOTANICAL NAME *Helichrysum bracteatum*

COMMON NAME Strawflower

RANGE Native to Western Australia. Tender annual.

HEIGHT Up to 5 feet; upright, bushy habit.

CULTURE Easy to grow in any well-drained loam soil in full sun. Start seed indoors at 60° to 70°F soil temperature and set out 6-week-old transplants, spaced 12 inches apart, after all danger of frost. Also can be direct-seeded.

DESCRIPTION Papery flowers are semi-double in white, yellow, orange, red, and pink. Dark green leaves are narrow, pointed. Popular as an accent in mixed beds and borders. Extremely popular for cutting to use in dried flower arrangements. Dwarf varieties, such as 'Dwarf Spangle' (12 inches tall) are good for edging and rock gardens.

BOTANICAL NAME *Hibiscus moscheutos*

COMMON NAME Southern Hibiscus

RANGE Native to Southern U.S. Hardy perennial best grown as tender annual.

HEIGHT Up to 5 feet; upright, branching habit.

CULTURE Prefers moist, fertile, humus-rich soil in full sun. Soak seed overnight to aid germination. Start seed indoors at 70° to 85°F soil temperature. Set out 8-week-old transplants, spaced at least 3 feet apart, after all danger of frost.

DESCRIPTION Spectacularly large flowers—up to 10 inches across—are white, pink, or red with contrasting crimson eyes and a consipicuous cluster of powdery yellow stamens. Dark green leaves are large and heart shaped. Popular as a tall background or massed in an island bed as a centerpiece. When frost kills the top growth in autumn, the roots will generally survive to produce new growth and flower the following spring.

BOTANICAL NAME *Hunnemannia fumariifolia*

COMMON NAME Mexican Tulip Poppy

RANGE Native to Mexico. Tender annual.

HEIGHT 2 feet; upright, branching habit.

CULTURE Easy to grow in any well-drained loam or sandy soil in full sun. Start seed indoors at 70° to 85°F and set out 4 to 5-week-old transplants, spaced 12 inches apart, after all danger of frost. Also can be direct-seeded. Drought resistant.

DESCRIPTION Shimmering yellow flowers are borne on slender stems. Dark green leaves are deeply indented. Popular accent in mixed beds and borders. Often included in meadow wildflower plantings.

BOTANICAL NAME *Iberis umbellata*

COMMON NAME Candytuft

RANGE Native to Spain. Hardy annual.

HEIGHT 12 inches; low, mounded habit.

CULTURE Easy to grow in any well-drained loam soil in full sun. Start seeds indoors at 60°F soil temperature and set out 6-week-old transplants, spaced 6 inches apart, several weeks before the last expected frost date. Also likes to be direct-seeded in early spring or late summer for fall blooms. Flowers best when nights are cool.

DESCRIPTION Clusters of dainty flowers form flat umbels in white, pink, and red. Dark green leaves are narrow, pointed. Popular for edging beds and borders. Dried seed pods are used in dried flower arrangements.

BOTANICAL NAME *Impatiens balsamina*

COMMON NAME Balsam

RANGE Native to India. Tender annual.

HEIGHT 2 to 3 feet; upright, bushy habit.

CULTURE Prefers moist, fertile, humus-rich soil in full sun or partial shade. Start seed indoors at 70° to 85°F and set out 6- to 8-week-old transplants, spaced 12 inches apart, after danger of frost.

DESCRIPTION Camellia-like flowers are mostly white, pink, red, and purple, in some varieties borne along the stems, in others on top of the foliage. Leaves are bright green, serrated, spear shaped. Suitable for massing in beds and borders.

BOTANICAL NAME *Impatiens wallerana*

COMMON NAME Patience plant

RANGE Native to Asia. Tender annual.

HEIGHT Up to 3 feet; bushy, spreading habit.

CULTURE Prefers moist, fertile, humus-rich soil in partial shade. Start seed indoors at 70° to 80°F and set out 10-week-old transplants, spaced 12 inches apart, after danger of frost.

DESCRIPTION Plants bloom continuously and are covered with single and double flowers, some varieties having solid colors and others possessing bicolored flowers. Leaves are dark green, broad, pointed. Popular for massing in beds and borders. Some varieties good for container planting, including hanging baskets. Dwarf varieties make sensational ground covers. Most widely planted flowering annual for shade.

RECOMMENDED VARIETIES 'Super Elfins' and 'Futura' grow just 12 inches high.

BOTANICAL NAME *Ipomoea alba*

COMMON NAME Moonflower

RANGE Native to South America. Tender annual.

HEIGHT Up to 10 feet; vining habit.

CULTURE Prefers moist, fertile, humus-rich soil in full sun. Start seeds indoors at 70° to 85°F. Soak seeds overnight to speed germination. Set out 6-week-old transplants, spaced 3 feet apart. Plants need strong support. Flowers open in the late afternoon, bloom at night, and close by noon the following day.

DESCRIPTION White trumpet-shaped flowers are borne on vining plants with dense foliage cover. Leaves are attractive, dark green, and heart shaped. Popular for decorating fences, trellises, and posts.

BOTANICAL NAME *Ipomoea tricolor*

COMMON NAME Morning Glory

RANGE Native to South America. Tender annual.

HEIGHT Up to 10 feet; vining habit.

CULTURE Easy to grow in any well-drained loam soil. Start seed at 70° to 85°F. Soak the hard-coated seeds overnight to aid germination. Set out 4-week-old transplants, spaced 3 feet apart, after danger of frost. Plants need strong support. Flowers open in the morning, generally close by afternoon except on cloudy days.

DESCRIPTION Wide trumpet-shaped flowers are mostly blue, white, red, pink, and bicolors. Leaves are dark green, heart shaped. Probably the most popular of all flowering vines, they climb by means of tendrils, making them suitable for covering fences, trellises, and posts.

RECOMMENDED VARIETY 'Heavenly Blue.'

BOTANICAL NAME *Kochia scoparia*

COMMON NAME Burning Bush

RANGE Native to Mexico. Tender annual.

HEIGHT 3 feet; bushy, upright habit.

CULTURE Easy to grow in any well-drained loam soil in full sun. Start seeds at 70° to 85°F and set out 4- to 6-week-old transplants, spaced 1 to 2 feet apart, after danger of frost.

DESCRIPTION Dense, feathery foliage forms an upright oval form resembling an Evergreen Cypress. Grown mostly for its bushy habit, it is popular for creating a hedge effect for beds and borders. Bright green summer foliage develops reddish tones in autumn.

BOTANICAL NAME *Lathyrus coloratus*

COMMON NAME Sweet Pea

RANGE Native to Sicily. Hardy annual.

HEIGHT Up to 6 feet; vining, upright habit.

CULTURE Prefers fertile, humus-rich, well-drained loam soil in full sun. Soak seeds overnight to aid germination and start them indoors at 60° to 75°F. Set out 4-week-old transplants, spaced 12 inches apart, several weeks before the last frost date. Can be direct-seeded where summers are cool. Flowers best when nights are cool. The tallest growing varieties need support.

DESCRIPTION Fragrant ruffled flowers with prominent keels are borne on strong vines with clover-like leaves and tendrils that allow the plants to climb. Tall kinds such as 'Galaxy' are popular for backgrounds in mixed beds and borders, also for decorating fences and trellises. Dwarf kinds such as 'Snoopea' do not need support (they possess no tendrils) and are useful for bedding in areas with cool summers. Sweet peas are among the finest flowers for cutting to make fresh flower arrangements.

BOTANICAL NAME *Lavatera trimestris*

COMMON NAME Rose-mallow

RANGE Native to the Mediterranean. Hardy annual.

HEIGHT Up to 3 feet; upright, bushy habit.

CULTURE Easy to grow in any well-drained loam soil in full sun. Start seed indoors at 70°F and set out 4-week-old transplants, spaced at least 12 inches apart, several weeks before the last frost date. Also can be direct-seeded.

DESCRIPTION The lovely hibiscus-like flowers with their shimmering petals are borne in such profusion that they almost completely hide the foliage. Colors include pink, white, and red. The dark green leaves resemble English ivy. Popular accent for mixed beds and borders. Also makes a spectacular temporary flowering hedge.

BOTANICAL NAME *Limnanthes douglasii*

COMMON NAME Scrambled Eggs, Meadow-foam

RANGE Native to California. Hardy annual.

HEIGHT 4 inches; low, ground-hugging habit.

CULTURE Easy to grow in any moist, well-drained loam soil in full sun. Plants tolerate crowding and direct-seeding is preferred. Seeds may be started at 60° to 70°F and set out 4-week-old transplants, spaced 6 inches apart, several weeks before the last frost date. Flowers best when nights are cool.

DESCRIPTION Dainty flowers are yellow in the middle with white petal edges. At peak bloom, the dazzling flowers are so numerous they completely hide the foliage. Mostly used as an edging for beds and borders; also as a temporary ground cover in areas with cool summers.

Here, an intensely planted bed of annuals features multiflora petunias, red verbena, and blue lobelia.

BOTANICAL NAME *Limonium sinuatum*

COMMON NAME Statice

RANGE Native to the Mediterranean. Tender annual.

HEIGHT 2 to 3 feet; upright, bushy habit.

CULTURE Easy to grow in any well-drained loam soil in full sun. Start seeds at 60° to 70°F soil temperature and set 8-week-old transplants, spaced 12 inches apart, after danger of frost.

DESCRIPTION Papery flower clusters are held erect on stiff stems. Color range includes white, yellow, pink, lavender, and blue. Leaves are lance-like. Suitable for mixed beds and borders. Popular for cutting and creating dried arrangements.

BOTANICAL NAME *Linaria maroccana*

COMMON NAME Toadflax

RANGE Native to Morocco. Hardy annual.

HEIGHT 12 inches; upright, spirelike habit.

CULTURE Easy to grow in any well-drained loam soil in full sun. Start seed indoors at 60°F and set out 6-week-old transplants, spaced 6 inches apart, several weeks before the last frost date. Tolerates crowding and usually is direct-seeded to make a drift of color.

DESCRIPTION Flowers resemble miniature snapdragons in white, yellow, pink, red, purple, and orange, plus bicolor. Leaves are bright green, slender, needlelike. Good for edging beds and borders. Suitable for rock gardens and wildflower meadows. Popular for cutting.

RECOMMENDED VARIETY 'Fairy Bouquet.'

BOTANICAL NAME *Lisianthus russulanus*
(Sometimes listed as Eustoma grandiflorum)

COMMON NAME Prairie Gentian

RANGE Native to Texas. Tender annual.

HEIGHT 1 to 2 feet; upright habit.

CULTURE Prefers a fertile, well-drained loam soil in full sun. Start seed indoors at 65° to 80°F soil temperature and set 8-to-10-week-old transplant, spaced 12 inches apart, after danger of frost. Pinch lead shoot after transplanting to encourage bushier habit.

DESCRIPTION Cup-shaped flowers are mostly blue, pink, or white. Leaves are blue-green, heart shaped, fleshy. A double form, Prima Donna, is available. Good accent for mixed beds and borders. Excellent for cutting. Good pot plant.

BOTANICAL NAME *Lobelia erinus*

COMMON NAME Lobelia erinus

RANGE Native to South Africa. Tender annual.

HEIGHT 6 inches; compact, mounded habit.

CULTURE Prefers fertile, moist, well-drained loam soil. Flowers best when nights are cool. Start seed at 70° to 80°F and set out 10-week-old transplants, spaced 6 inches apart, after all danger of frost.

DESCRIPTION Dainty flowers are borne in profusion on airy plants. Colors include blue, rose pink, red, and white. Bright green leaves are small, needlelike. Popular as an edging for beds and borders. Excellent for hanging baskets and other containers.

RECOMMENDED VARIETY 'Blue Heaven.'

BOTANICAL NAME *Lobularia maritima*

COMMON NAME Alyssum

RANGE Native to the Mediterranean. Hardy annual.

HEIGHT 6 inches; low, mounded, spreading habit.

CULTURE Easy to grow in any well-drained loam soil in full sun. Tolerates crowding and is most often direct-seeded. If transplanting is preferred, start seed at 60° to 70°F and set out 4-week-old transplants, spaced 6 inches apart, several weeks before the last expected frost date.

DESCRIPTION Masses of dainty white, pink, or purple flowers are borne in such profusion they often completely hide the foliage. Bright green leaves are small, narrow, pointed. Extremely popular as an edging for beds and borders. Also good for hanging baskets and other container plantings. Grows among paving stones and along dry walls.

RECOMMENDED VARIETIES 'Carpet of Snow' (white) and 'Wonderland' (deep pink).

BOTANICAL NAME *Machaeranthera tanacetifolia*

COMMON NAME Tahoka-daisy

RANGE Native to Texas. Hardy annual.

HEIGHT 1 to 2 feet; low, bushy habit.

CULTURE Easy to grow in any well-drained loam soil in full sun. Start seed at 60°F soil temperature and set out 6-week-old transplants, spaced 12 inches apart, several weeks before the last expected frost date.

DESCRIPTION Blue flowers have golden yellow centers, resemble Michaelmas Daisies. Leaves are bright green, deeply indented. Good accent for mixed beds and borders. Popular for rock gardens. Suitable for cutting.

BOTANICAL NAME *Matthiola incana*

COMMON NAME Stocks

RANGE Native to Southern Europe. Hardy Annual.

HEIGHT 3 feet; erect, spirelike habit.

CULTURE Prefers moist, fertile, humus-rich soil in full sun. Start seed at 65° to 75°F soil temperature, but after seeds germinate plants should not be subjected to air temperatures higher than 65°F. If plants are exposed to temperatures any higher than 65°F they are unlikely to bloom. Set out 6-week-old transplants, spaced 12 inches apart, several weeks before the last expected frost date. Pinch lead shoot to encourage side branching.

DESCRIPTION Fragrant, ruffled flowers are studded in a column along strong stems. Colors include white, yellow, pink, red, and purple. Leaves are straplike. Popular for beds and borders where 4 to 5 months of cool temperatures prevail. Excellent for cutting.

RECOMMENDED VARIETY '7-Weeks Tyrsomic,' early flowering.

RELATED SPECIES M. Bicornis ('Night-Scented Stocks').

BOTANICAL NAME *Mimulus* x hybridus

COMMON NAME Monkey Flower

RANGE Native to Chile. Hardy annual.

HEIGHT 12 inches; low, mounded habit.

CULTURE Prefers moist, fertile, humus-rich soil in sun or partial shade. Start seed at 60°F soil temperature and set out 8- to 10-week-old transplants, spaced 6 to 12 inches apart, several weeks before the last expected frost date. Flowers best during cool weather.

DESCRIPTION Tubular flowers have heavily freckled faces and a velvety texture. Colors include white, yellow, orange, red, and pink. Leaves are broad, serrated, bright green. Suitable for massing in beds and borders. Good for container planting, especially beside garden pools.

BOTANICAL NAME *Mirabilis jalapa*

COMMON NAME Four-o'-clock

RANGE Native to Peru. Perennials grown as tender annuals.

HEIGHT 3 feet; bushy habit.

CULTURE Easy to grow in any well-drained loam or sandy soil in full sun. Start seed at 70° to 85°F and set out 6-week-old transplants, spaced 1 to 2 feet apart, after danger of frost. Also can be direct-seeded.

DESCRIPTION Tubular flowers bloom continuously all summer; they stay closed during the morning on sunny days, but remain open all day on cloudy days. Colors are variable from plant to plant and on individual plants; a single flower may have white, yellow, orange, and pink blossoms, some of them even bicolored. Leaves are heart shaped. Popular accent for mixed beds and borders.

BOTANICAL NAME *Moluccella laevis*

COMMON NAME Bells-of-Ireland

RANGE Native to Asia. Tender annual.

HEIGHT 2 to 3 feet; bushy, spreading habit.

CULTURE Easy to grow in any well-drained loam soil. Soak seeds overnight to aid germination, and start them at 70° to 85°F. Set out 6 to 8-week-old transplants, spaced 12 inches apart, after danger of frost. Also can be direct-seeded after danger of frost.

DESCRIPTION Slender flower spikes are crowded with ornamental, bell-shaped, green flower bracts. Leaves are broad, indented. Popular accent in beds and borders. Valued for cutting and dried flower arrangements.

BOTANICAL NAME *Myosotis sylvatica*

COMMON NAME Forget-me-not

RANGE Native to Europe. Biennial grown as hardy annual.

HEIGHT 12 inches; low, mounded habit.

CULTURE Prefers moist, fertile loam soil in sun or partial shade. Start seed at 70°F and set out 8-week-old transplants, spaced 6 to 12 inches apart, several weeks before the last expected frost date. Flowers best when nights are cool.

DESCRIPTION Dainty, blue, star-shaped flowers cover the plants in early summer. Leaves are dark green, straplike. Popular for edging beds and borders, also for massing along pond margins and stream banks. Plants reseed themselves readily. A bed of Forget-me-nots mixed with tulips make a particularly effective planting combination.

BOTANICAL NAME *Nemesia strumosa*

COMMON NAME Nemesia

RANGE Native to South Africa. Tender annual.

HEIGHT 12 inches; mounded habit.

CULTURE Prefers moist, fertile, well-drained loam soil in full sun. Start seed at 60°F and set out 6- to 8-week old transplants, spaced 12 inches apart. Flowers best when nights are cool.

DESCRIPTION Orchid-like flowers, arranged in clusters, have a prominent lower lip. Colors include yellow, red, white, pink, and orange. Leaves are narrow, pointed. Popular for massing in beds and borders in areas with cool summers. Good for containers. A blue Nemesia, 'Blue Gem,' is grown separately and not generally included in seed mixtures.

BOTANICAL NAME *Nemophila menziesii*

COMMON NAME Baby-Blue-Eyes

RANGE Native to California. Hardy annual.

HEIGHT 9 inches; low, mounded habit.

CULTURE Easy to grow in any well-drained loam soil in full sun. Start seed at 60°F and set out 6-week-old transplants, spaced 6 inches apart, several weeks before the last expected frost date. Also can be direct-seeded. Flowers best when nights are cool.

DESCRIPTION Dainty, cup-shaped blue flowers have white centers. Bright green leaves are delicate, fern-like. Good edging for beds and borders. Popular for rock gardens and growing in wildflower meadow mixtures. Self-seeds readily.

BOTANICAL NAME *Nicotiana alata*

COMMON NAME Flowering Tobacco

RANGE Native to South America. Tender annual.

HEIGHT 3 feet; erect, bushy habit.

CULTURE Easy to grow in any well-drained loam soil in full sun. Start seed indoors at 70° to 85°F and set out 8-week-old transplants, spaced 12 inches apart, after all danger of frost.

DESCRIPTION Borne in profusion on long stems, the tubular flowers can be white, pink, red, yellow, or green. Leaves are dark green, oval. Popular for massing as a background in mixed beds and borders.

RECOMMENDED VARIETY 'Nicki' hybrids, a semi-dwarf strain growing 18 inches high that does not close up in the afternoon like other varieties.

BOTANICAL NAME *Nierembergia hippomanica*

COMMON NAME Cupflower

RANGE Native to South America. Perennial best grown as tender annual.

HEIGHT 12 inches; low, mounded habit.

CULTURE Easy to grow in any well-drained loam soil in full sun. Start seeds at 70° to 85°F and set out 10-week-old transplants, spaced 6 inches apart, after all danger of frost.

DESCRIPTION Small cup-shaped purple flowers are produced in such abundance they almost hide the foliage, which is delicate and needlelike. Good for edging beds and borders. Popular as a flowering pot plant.

BOTANICAL NAME *Nolana napiformis*

COMMON NAME Nolana

RANGE Native to Peru and Chile. Tender annual.

HEIGHT 4 to 12 inches; low, mounded habit.

CULTURE Easy to grow in any well-drained loam soil. Start seeds at 70° to 85° F and set out 6-week old transplants, spaced 12 inches apart, after all danger of frost, in full sun.

DESCRIPTION A creeping plant that covers itself in cheerful blue flowers with yellow and white throats, resembling small morning glories. Soft, fleshy green leaves are indented. Good to use for edging and as a temporary ground cover.

This mixed bed of annuals features silvery dusty miller, red scarlet sage, blue and pink lisianthus, an assortment of nicotiana, and a mixture of zinnias.

BOTANICAL NAME *Papaver nudicaule*

COMMON NAME Iceland Poppy

RANGE Native to Canada. Hardy annual.

HEIGHT 3 feet; erect habit.

CULTURE Easy to grow in any well-drained loam soil in full sun. Flowers best when nights are cool. Direct-seeding is generally preferred since transplants are subject to shock. Even where plants generally grow better from direct-seeding, some gardeners still prefer to transplant. In this case, start seed at 55° to 65°F and set out 4-week-old transplants, spaced 12 inches apart, several weeks before the last expected frost date in spring.

DESCRIPTION Flowers are mostly orange, yellow, pink, and white on slender, wiry stems. Bright green leaves are serrated, forming a rosette. Good accent for beds and borders. Popular for wildflower meadows. Excellent cut flower, especially when cut stems are held over a flame to seal them and prevent wilting.

BOTANICAL NAME *Papaver rhoeas*

COMMON NAME Shirley Poppy

RANGE Native to Europe. Hardy annual.

HEIGHT 3 feet; upright, clump-forming habit.

CULTURE Easy to grow in any well-drained loam or sandy soil in full sun. Direct-seeding is generally preferred since plants tolerate crowding. Even though plants grow better from direct-seeding, some gardeners still prefer to transplant. In this case, start seeds at 60° to 70°F and set out 4-week-old transplants, spaced 12 inches apart, several weeks before the last expected frost date.

DESCRIPTION Flowers are mostly red, white, and pink with black markings at the base of each petal, growing on top of wiry stems. Leaves are hairy, serrated. Popular as accents in beds and borders, also for wildflower meadows. Suitable for cutting if cut stems are held over a flame immediately after picking to seal the ends and prevent wilting.

BOTANICAL NAME *Pelargonium* x *hortorum*

COMMON NAME Geranium

RANGE Native to South Africa. Perennial best grown as tender annual.

HEIGHT 12 inches; erect habit.

CULTURE Easy to grow in any well-drained loam soil in full sun. Start seed at 70° to 85°F and set out 8- to 10-week-old transplants, spaced 12 inches apart, after danger of frost.

DESCRIPTION Flowers are borne in clusters on strong, slender stems. Color ranges from red, pink, and salmon to white and bicolors. Leaves are usually brown around the margin and rounded with ruffled edges. Popular for massing in beds and borders. Suitable for containers.

RECOMMENDED VARIETY 'Orbits,' an early flowering dwarf strain with conspicuous leaf-zone patterns and a natural tendency to branch freely from the base.

BOTANICAL NAME *Penstemon gloxinioides*

COMMON NAME Bearded Tongue

RANGE Native to Mexico. Perennial best treated as tender annual.

HEIGHT 2 feet; erect, spirelike habit.

CULTURE Easy to grow in any well-drained loam soil in full sun. Start seed at 60°F and set out 8- to 10-week-old transplants, spaced 12 inches apart, after all danger of frost. Flowers best when nights are cool.

DESCRIPTION Tubular flowers form long spikes. Color range includes white, red, pink, and purple. Leaves are bright green, lancelike. Useful accent in beds and borders. Good for cutting.

RECOMMENDED VARIETY 'Giant Floradale' has large flowers.

BRADFORD WG LIBRARY
100 HOLLAND COURT, BOX 130
BRADFORD, ONT. L3Z 2A7

BOTANICAL NAME *Petunia* x *hybrida*

COMMON NAME Petunia

RANGE Native to South America. Tender annual.

HEIGHT 12 inches; mounded habit.

CULTURE Easy to grow in any well-drained loam soil in full sun. Start seeds at 70° to 85°F and set out 8- to 10-week-old transplants, spaced 12 inches apart, after all danger of frost.

DESCRIPTION Two types are most popular among home gardeners: 'multi-floras' have relatively small and numerous flowers, and 'grandifloras' with their large, ruffled flowers. Color range includes red, white, blue, yellow, pink, purple, and bicolors. Popular for massing in beds and borders. Good for hanging baskets and other kinds of containers.

BOTANICAL NAME *Phlox drummondii*

COMMON NAME Phlox

RANGE Native to Texas. Hardy annual.

HEIGHT 12 inches; low, spreading habit.

CULTURE Easy to grow in any well-drained loam soil in full sun. Start seed at 55° to 65°F and set out 6- to 8-week-old transplants, spaced 12 inches apart, several weeks before the last expected frost date in spring. Flowers best when nights are cool.

DESCRIPTION Flowers are produced in clusters on short stems. Colors include red, white, pink, and purple plus bicolors. Leaves are bright green, spear shaped. Popular for massing in beds and borders, also rock gardens.

RECOMMENDED VARIETY 'Twinkle' mixed colors, a dwarf with pointed petals.

BOTANICAL NAME *Portulaca grandiflora*

COMMON NAME Moss Rose

RANGE Native to South America. Tender annual.

HEIGHT 6 inches; low, spreading habit.

CULTURE Easy to grow in any well-drained sandy or loam soil in full sun. Start seeds at 70° to 85°F and set out 4-week-old transplants, spaced 12 inches apart, after all danger of frost. Also can be direct-seeded.

DESCRIPTION Shimmering rose-like flowers are borne in profusion on succulent plants. Bright green leaves are narrow, plump, pointed. Color range includes red, white, yellow, orange, and purple. Popular for edging beds and borders. Also suitable for window boxes and other container plantings.

RECOMMENDED VARIETY 'Calypso' hybrid mixed colors, containing a high percentage of double flowers that remain open all day.

BOTANICAL NAME *Reseda odorata*

COMMON NAME Mignonette

RANGE Native to Egypt. Hardy annual.

HEIGHT 12 inches; erect, bushy habit.

CULTURE Easy to grow in any well-drained loam soil in full sun. Start seed at 70° to 85°F and set out 6-week-old transplants, spaced 6 inches apart, several weeks before the last expected frost date of spring. Also can be direct-seeded.

DESCRIPTION Fragrant orange flowers cluster, forming an inconspicuous, though not very ornamental, flower spike. The heavy, pleasant fragrance is reason enough to find a small spot for it in mixed beds and borders. Good for cutting. A good choice for window boxes.

BOTANICAL NAME *Ricinus communis*

COMMON NAME Castor Bean Plant

RANGE Native to Africa. Perennial grown as tender annual.

HEIGHT Up to 8 feet; erect, branching habit.

CULTURE Easy to grow in any well-drained loam soil in full sun. Start seed at 70° to 85°F soil temperature and set out 6-week-old transplants, spaced at least 3 feet apart, after danger of frost.

DESCRIPTION Grown for its spectacular tropical foliage. Gigantic, glossy, deeply indented leaves can measure up to 3 feet across. Creates a dramatic accent in beds and borders, particularly island beds and foundation plantings. The bean-size seeds have speckled markings and are used to make necklaces. Caution: seeds and other parts are poisonous.

BOTANICAL NAME *Rudbeckia hirta burpeeii*

COMMON NAME Gloriosa Daisy; Black-eyed Susan

RANGE Native to North America. Perennial grown as hardy annual.

HEIGHT 3 feet; erect, branching habit.

CULTURE Easy to grow in any well-drained loam soil in full sun. Start seed at 65° to 75°F and set out 8-week-old transplants, spaced 12 inches apart, several weeks before the last expected frost date of spring. Also can be direct-seeded.

DESCRIPTION Large, daisy-like flowers can be single or double. Color range includes yellow, orange, and mahogany plus bicolors, all with contrasting black or green eyes, depending on variety. Popular for massing in beds and borders, also for wildflower meadows.

RECOMMENDED VARIETIES 'Double Gold,' spectacular yellow double flower excellent for backgrounds and 'Marmalade,' a single-flowered orange dwarf that flowers abundantly, just 12 inches high.

BOTANICAL NAME *Salpiglossis sinuata*

COMMON NAME Painted Tongue; Velvet Flower

RANGE Native to South America. Tender annual.

HEIGHT 3 feet; upright, bushy habit.

CULTURE Prefers a fertile, well-drained, humus-rich soil in full sun. Start seed at 70° to 85°F and set out 8-week-old transplants, spaced 12 inches apart, after all danger of frost. Flowers best when nights are cool.

DESCRIPTION Petunia-like flowers have an incredibly diverse color range including red, white, blue, purple, pink, yellow, and brown, usually with conspicuous petal veins and contrasting freckles. Bright green leaves are pointed, notched. Good accent for mixed beds and borders where summers are cool. Popular pot plant for the greenhouse and conservatory.

BOTANICAL NAME *Salvia farinacea*

COMMON NAME Blue Salvia

RANGE Native to Texas. Perennial grown as tender annual.

HEIGHT 3 feet; upright, bushy habit.

CULTURE Easy to grow in any well-drained loam soil in sun or partial shade. Start seed at 70°F and set out 8-week-old transplants, spaced 12 inches apart, after all danger of frost. Drought resistant.

DESCRIPTION Small florets form erect flower spikes on slender stems. Favored color is blue though white is also available. Leaves are dark green or gray-green, spear shaped. Valuable for backgrounds in mixed beds and borders.

RECOMMENDED VARIETY 'Catima,' an intense, deep blue.

A beautiful free-form lawn surrounded by borders of annuals. Salvia 'Evening Glow' flowers prolifically in the foreground.

BOTANICAL NAME *Salvia splendens*

COMMON NAME Scarlet Sage

RANGE Native to South America. Tender annual.

HEIGHT 1 to 3 feet; bushy habit.

CULTURE Easy to grow in any well-drained garden loam in sun or partial shade. Start seed at 70° to 85°F and set out 8-week-old transplants, spaced 12 inches apart, after all danger of frost. Flowers best when nights are cool.

DESCRIPTION Tubular florets are arranged into a spectacular flower spike. Favored color is red, though pink, white, and purple are available. Dark green leaves are spear shaped. Extremely popular for massing in beds and borders, also for container growing.

RECOMMENDED VARIETY 'Carabiniere,' an intense fiery red with solid spikes that grow 12 inches high.

BOTANICAL NAME *Sanvitalia procumbens*

COMMON NAME Creeping Zinnia

RANGE Native to Mexico. Tender annual.

HEIGHT 6 inches; low, spreading habit.

CULTURE Easy to grow in well-drained loam soil in full sun. Start seed at 70° to 85°F and set out 4-week-old transplants, spaced 12 inches apart, after all danger of frost. Also can be direct-seeded.

DESCRIPTION Dainty daisy-like flowers are bright yellow with black centers. Leaves are bright green, spear shaped. Creates a beautiful ground cover. Popular for edging beds and borders. Suitable for window boxes and rock gardens since plants will cascade.

BOTANICAL NAME *Scabiosa atropurpurea*

COMMON NAME Sweet Scabious; Pincushion Flower

RANGE Native to Europe. Hardy annual.

HEIGHT 3 feet; erect, branching habit.

CULTURE Easy to grow in any well-drained loam soil in full sun. Start seed at 70°F and set out 4- to 5-week-old transplants, spaced 12 inches apart, in mid-April.

DESCRIPTION Flowers resemble tight pincushions, rounded and fully double. Colors include blue, white, red, pink, and black. Good accent for mixed beds and borders. Excellent for cutting.

RECOMMENDED VARIETY 'Giant Imperial.'

BOTANICAL NAME *Schizanthus* x *wisetonensis*

COMMON NAME Butterfly Flower; Poor Man's Orchid

RANGE Native to Chile. Tender annual.

HEIGHT 2 feet; upright, bushy habit.

CULTURE Prefers fertile, well-drained, humus-rich soil in full sun. Start seed at 60° to 70°F and set out 10- to 12-week-old transplants, spaced 12 inches apart, several weeks before the last expected frost date. The taller varieties may need staking. Flowers best when nights are cool.

DESCRIPTION Orchid-like flowers are clustered into a long flower spike held erect on slender stems. Color range includes white, yellow, orange, pink, and purple, usually with freckled throats. Good for massing in beds and borders where summers are cool and moist. Popular for growing as a flowering pot plant in greenhouses and conservatories.

RECOMMENDED VARIETY 'Hit Parade,' a compact dwarf growing just 12 inches high; excellent for bedding.

BOTANICAL NAME *Senecio cineraria*

COMMON NAME Dusty Miller

RANGE Native to the Mediterranean. Perennial grown as tender annual.

HEIGHT 12 inches; low, mounded habit.

CULTURE Easy to grow in any well-drained loam soil in full sun. Start seed at 60° to 70°F and set out 10-week-old transplants, spacing them 6 inches apart, after danger of frost.

DESCRIPTION One of several plant species commonly called 'Dusty Miller,' grown purely for the ornamental value of their silvery gray indented leaves. Extremely popular for edging beds and borders and combining with other plants in containers.

RECOMMENDED VARIETY 'Silverdust,' which displays finely indented, velvetlike leaves.

BOTANICAL NAME *Tagetes erecta*

COMMON NAME American Marigold; African Marigold

RANGE Native to Mexico. Tender annual.

HEIGHT Up to 3 feet; erect, bushy habit.

CULTURE Easy to grow in any well-drained loam soil in full sun. Start seed at 70° to 85°F and set out 6-week-old transplants, spaced 12 inches apart, after all danger of frost. Also can be direct-seeded.

DESCRIPTION Flowers are mostly double in yellow, orange, gold, and white. Leaves are feathery, with a spicy fragrance, though odorless kinds are available. Popular for massing in beds and borders. Good for cutting.

RECOMMENDED VARIETY 'First Lady,' a primrose-yellow, semi-dwarf.

BOTANICAL NAME *Tagetes patula*

COMMON NAME French Marigold

RANGE Native to Mexico. Tender annual.

HEIGHT 12 inches; low, mounded habit.

CULTURE Easy to grow in any well-drained loam soil in full sun. Start seed at 70° to 85°F and set out 6-week-old transplants, spaced 12 inches apart, after danger of frost. Also can be direct-seeded.

DESCRIPTION Flowers can be single or double, the doubles often featuring a crest—a raised center of petals. Color range includes yellow, orange, red, and gold. Leaves are feathery and have a spicy odor that repels many insects. Popular for massing in beds and borders, also for edging paths. Good for container plantings, especially window boxes.

RECOMMENDED VARIETY 'Boy' series. A cross between the dwarf French and tall American called 'Triploid hybrids' is an exceptional class of dwarf marigold that is free flowering.

BOTANICAL NAME *Tagetes tenuifolia*

COMMON NAME Striped Marigold

RANGE Native to Mexico. Tender annual.

HEIGHT 12 inches; cushionlike habit.

CULTURE Easy to grow in any well-drained loam soil in full sun. Start seeds at 70° to 85°F and set out 6-week-old transplants, spaced 12 inches apart, after all danger of frost. Also can be direct-seeded.

DESCRIPTION Dainty daisy-like flowers are mostly yellow, orange, or rusty red, borne in such profusion they almost completely hide the foliage. Leaves are finely cut, fern-like, and have a spicy odor that repels many insects. Mostly used for edging beds and borders. Also good for containers and rock gardens.

RECOMMENDED VARIETIES 'Lemon Gem' (lemon yellow) and 'Paprika' (rusty red with yellow center).

BOTANICAL NAME *Thunbergia alata*

COMMON NAME Black-eyed Susan Vine

RANGE Native to Africa. Tender annual.

HEIGHT Up to 10 feet; vining habit.

CULTURE Easy to grow in any well-drained loam soil in full sun. Start seed at 70° to 85°F and set out 6-week-old transplants, spaced 12 inches apart, after danger of frost. Also can be direct-seeded.

DESCRIPTION Mostly orange flowers have black eyes. Bright green leaves are broad, pointed. Good to cover fences and climb up trellises. A dwarf strain, 'Susie,' is especially suitable for hanging baskets and window boxes and is available in orange, yellow, and white (all with black eyes).

BOTANICAL NAME *Tithonia rotundifolia*

COMMON NAME Mexican Sunflower

RANGE Native to Mexico. Tender annual.

HEIGHT 5 feet; erect, branching habit.

CULTURE Easy to grow in any well-drained loam soil in full sun. Start seed at 70° to 85°F and set out 6-week-old transplants, spaced at least 12 inches apart, after all danger of frost. Also can be direct-seeded.

DESCRIPTION Dahlia-like flowers are bright orange. Dark green leaves are broad, pointed, serrated. Useful background for beds and borders. Can create a hedge effect with its thick foliage cover. Good cut flower if cut in bud stage.

BOTANICAL NAME *Torenia fournieri*

COMMON NAME Wishbone Flower

RANGE Native to North Africa. Tender annual.

HEIGHT 12 inches; low, mounded habit.

CULTURE Prefers fertile, moist, humus-rich soil in partial shade. Start seeds at 70° to 85°F and set out 10-week-old transplants, spaced 8 inches apart, after all danger of frost.

DESCRIPTION Flowers resemble small pansies with an unusual arrangement of stamens in the throat in the shape of a wishbone. Colors are mostly violet-blue and pink. Leaves are bright green, serrated. Popular for edging beds and borders. Also grown as a flowering pot plant.

BOTANICAL NAME *Tropaeolum majus*

COMMON NAME Nasturtium

RANGE Native to South America. Hardy annual.

HEIGHT 12 inches; low, spreading habit.

CULTURE Easy to grow in any well-drained loam soil in full sun. Start seed at 65°F and set out 5- to 6-week-old transplants, spaced 12 inches apart, several weeks before the last expected frost date in spring. Flowers best when nights are cool. Can be trained to climb. Also can be direct-seeded.

DESCRIPTION Flowers can be single- or double-flowered, with or without spurs. Plants with spurless flowers (such as 'Whirlybird') tend to display better because the flowers always face up. Color range includes red, yellow, orange, apricot, white, pink, and mahogany. Leaves are shaped like parasols. Suitable for low beds and borders, also containers. Tall kinds can be used to cover trellises and fences.

BOTANICAL NAME *Venidium fastuosum*

COMMON NAME Monarch-of-the-veldt

RANGE Native to South Africa. Tender annual.

HEIGHT 2 feet; bushy habit.

CULTURE Easy to grow in any well-drained loam soil in full sun. Start seed at 70° to 80°F and set out 6-week-old transplants, spaced 12 inches apart, after danger of frost. Also can be direct-seeded. Flowers best when nights are cool.

DESCRIPTION Daisy-like, semi-double flowers are golden yellow with a black center encircled by an attractive brown zone. Bright green leaves are serrated. Good accent for beds and borders. Excellent for cutting.

BOTANICAL NAME *Verbena* x *hybrida*

COMMON NAME Summer Verbena

RANGE Native to South America. Tender annual.

HEIGHT 12 inches; low, spreading habit.

CULTURE Easy to grow in any well-drained loam soil in full sun. Start seed at 70° to 85°F and set out 8-week-old transplants, spaced 12 inches apart, after all danger of frost.

DESCRIPTION Primrose-like florets are arranged in flat clusters. Color range includes white, red, pink, blue, and purple with white centers. Leaves are dark green, narrow, serrated. Popular for massing in beds and borders, and for edging. Suitable for containers, especially window boxes.

RECOMMENDED VARIETY 'Springtime,' a good mixture that branches freely.

BOTANICAL NAME *Viola tricolor*

COMMON NAME Pansy

RANGE Native to Europe. Biennial grown as an annual.

HEIGHT 8 inches; low, mounded habit.

CULTURE Prefers moist, fertile, humus-rich soil in sun or partial shade. Start seed at 70°F and set out 10-week-old transplants, spaced 6 inches apart, either in fall or several weeks before the last expected spring frost date. Flowers best when nights are cool.

DESCRIPTION Cheerful flowers often have markings that resemble human facial characteristics. Color range includes red, white, blue, yellow, and orange with black blotches or black "whiskers," depending on the variety. Extremely popular for massing in beds and borders for early spring bloom. Also suitable for containers (especially window boxes) and rock gardens.

RECOMMENDED VARIETY 'Majestic Giants' or any hybrid mixture since hybrids are earliest-flowering and heat-resistant.

BOTANICAL NAME *Xeranthemum annuum*

COMMON NAME Immortelle

RANGE Native to the Mediterranean. Hardy annual.

HEIGHT 2 feet; erect habit.

CULTURE Easy to grow in any well-drained loam soil in full sun. Start seed at 70° to 85°F and set out 6-week-old transplants, spaced 12 inches apart, several weeks before the last expected spring frost date. Also can be direct-seeded.

DESCRIPTION Papery flowers have pointed petals. Colors include pink and white. Good accent for mixed beds and borders. Mostly grown for cutting and dried flower arrangements.

BOTANICAL NAME *Zinnia angustifolia*

COMMON NAME Classic Zinnia

RANGE Native to Mexico. Tender annual.

HEIGHT 12 inches; spreading habit.

CULTURE Easy to grow in any well-drained loam soil in full sun. Start seed at 70° to 85°F and set out 4-week-old transplants, spaced 12 inches apart, after danger of frost. Also can be direct-seeded. Tolerates dry soil.

DESCRIPTION Small, single orange flowers are borne in profusion on low-growing, ground-hugging plants. Leaves are smooth, pointed. Popular for edging beds and borders and as a ground cover to decorate dry slopes. Good for containers, particularly window boxes.

BOTANICAL NAME *Zinnia elegans*

COMMON NAME Zinnia

RANGE Native to Mexico. Tender annual.

HEIGHT Up to 3 feet; upright, branching habit.

CULTURE Easy to grow in any well-drained loam soil in full sun. Start seed at 70° to 85°F and set out 4- to 5-week-old transplants, spaced 12 inches apart, after danger of frost. Also can be direct-seeded.

DESCRIPTION Flowers are mostly divided into two kinds: dahlia-flowered with rounded petals and cactus-flowered with quilled petals. Color range includes white, yellow, orange, red, pink, purple, and green, plus bicolors. Popular massed in beds and borders. Good for cutting. Special dwarf varieties, such as the 'Peter Pans' are best for bedding.

Opposite page: This water garden features beds of impatiens radiating out from a circular pool in a "cartwheel" design.
Above right: Mixed beds featuring both annuals and perennials.
Below right: Pink petunias and golden yellow marigolds make an effective color combination.

CHAPTER THREE

GARDEN PLANS

THE FOLLOWING SECTION ILLUSTRATES several versions of annual garden design, with planting suggestions for both sun and shade. Some of the color schemes are bright and bold, others are soft for a more old-fashioned look. The patterns are inspired by traditional knot gardens, with planting spaces outlined in dwarf shrubs like boxwood. To create a parterre garden, simply use an edging of brick, stone, or lumber. All of these designs can be modified to create a square, circle, oval, or narrow rectangular space.

When laying out the pattern, mark the sections with string and stakes, first getting the corners properly placed and square, and then the center point. The pathways can be paved with brick, flagstone, or crushed gravel for permanence, or with organic mulch such as wood chips or tan bark.

The annuals chosen to be planted in full sun will not only produce an attractive outdoor display, but they will also yield flowers for cutting to create beautiful arrangements.

The butterfly garden is not only laid out in the shape of a butterfly, but the annuals selected will also attract butterflies. This garden is especially effective if it can be admired from a high elevation, such as a terrace, deck, or bedroom window.

Another set of designs, featuring selections for both sun and shade, shows what can be accomplished with a simple island bed. These have been laid out in a rectangular shape, but are easily adapted to either a square or round shape. These beds look especially effective as lawn highlights.

ISLAND BED; RECTANGLE WITH BULL'S-EYES

SUN

1—Gray dusty miller *(Senecio cineraria)*
2—Red salvia *(Salvia splendens)* or zinnia *(Zinnia elegans)*
3—Gold marigold *(Tagetes erecta)*, calendula *(Calendula officinalis)*, or crested celosia *(Celosia cristata)*
4—Blue salvia *(Salvia farinacea)* or blue ageratum *(Ageratum houstonianum)*
5—Hot pink zinnia *(Zinnia elegans)*, aster *(Callistephus chinensis)*, petunia *(Petunia x hybrida)*, or cosmos *(Cosmos bipinnatus)*

SHADE

1—White impatiens *(Impatiens wallerana)*
2—Scarlet impatiens *(Impatiens wallerana)* or red wax begonia *(Begonia x semperflorens)*
3—Mimulus *(Mimulus x hybridus)*, apricot viola *(Viola tricolor)*, Chinese forget-me-not *(Cynoglossum amabile)*
4—Blue browallia *(Browallia speciosa)*, viola *(Viola tricolor,* or Chinese forget-me-not *(Cynoglossum amabile)*
5—Hot pink impatiens *(Impatiens wallerana)*

Left: Shown here is a good companion planting featuring scarlet sage and dusty miller.

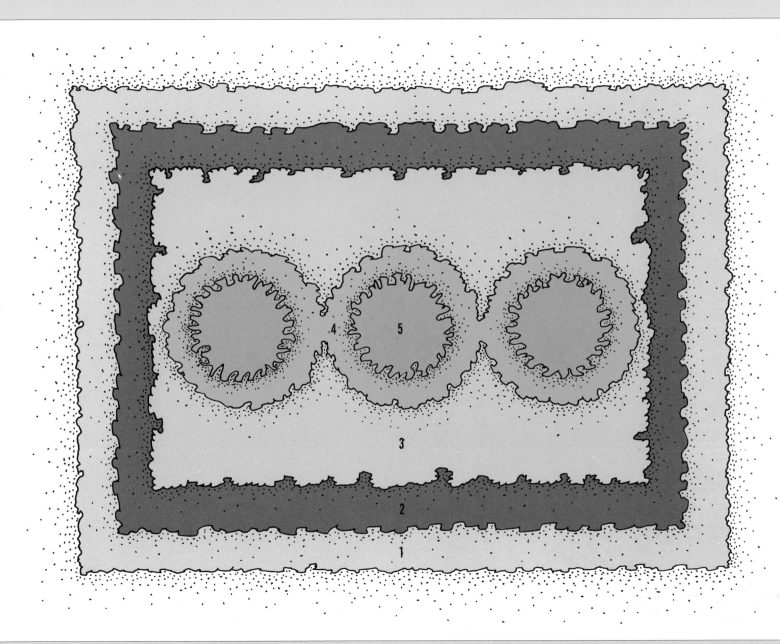

A. M. Georgens

ISLAND BED; RECTANGLE

SUN

1—Dusty miller *(Senecio cineraria)* or white geranium *(Pelargonium* x *hortorum)*
2—Blue petunia *(Petunia* x *hybrida),* ageratum *(Ageratum houstonianum),* pansies *(Viola tricolor),* or blue salvia *(Salvia farinacea)*
3—Blue canterbury bells *(Campanula media),* delphinium *(Delphinium elatum),* or larkspur *(Consolida ambigua)*
4—White cosmos *(Cosmos bipinnatus)*

SHADE

1—White impatiens *(Impatiens wallerana)*
2—Forget-me-not *(Myosotis sylvatica),* viola *(Viola tricolor),* or cambridge blue lobelia *(Lobelia erinus)*
3—Deep blue browallia *(Browallia speciosa)* or crystal palace lobelia *(Lobelia erinus)*
4—White foxglove *(Digitalis purpurea)*

Left: White and blue salvia farinacea mixed with red celosia create an informal effect against mass plantings of white and yellow gazania.

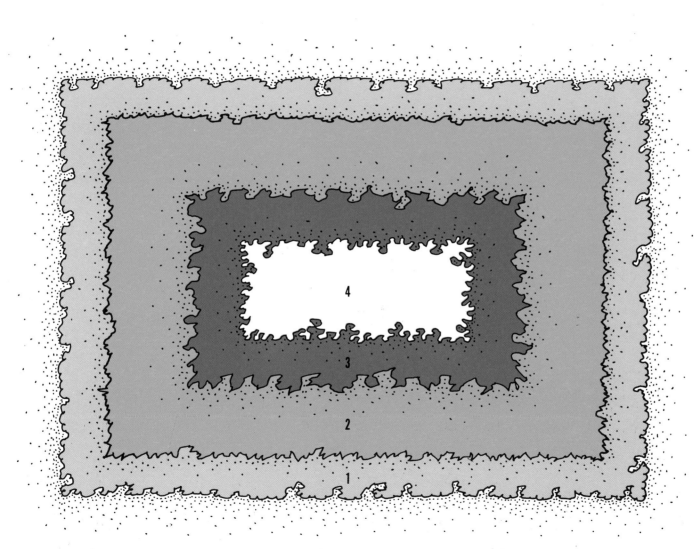

A. M. Georgens

ISLAND BED; RECTANGLE

SUN

1—Gray dusty miller *(Senecio cineraria)*
2—Peach: geranium *(Pelargonium* x *hortorum)*
3—Pink: geranium *(Pelargonium* x *hortorum)* or aster *(Callistephus chinensis)*, Shirley poppies *(Papaver rhoeas)*, or petunias *(Petunia* x *hybrida)*
4—White: cosmos *(Cosmos bipinnatus)* or hollyhocks *(Alcea rosea)*, stock *(Matthiola incana)* or delphinium *(Delphinium elatum)*

SHADE

1—White: impatiens *(Impatiens wallerana)*
2—Peach: impatiens *(Impatiens wallerana)*
3—Pink: impatiens *(Impatiens wallerana)* or coleus *(Coleus* x *hybridus)*
4—White: impatiens *(Impatiens wallerana)*

Left: Here, a bed of impatiens is used as an edging between the lawn and a brick path, with hanging baskets in the background.

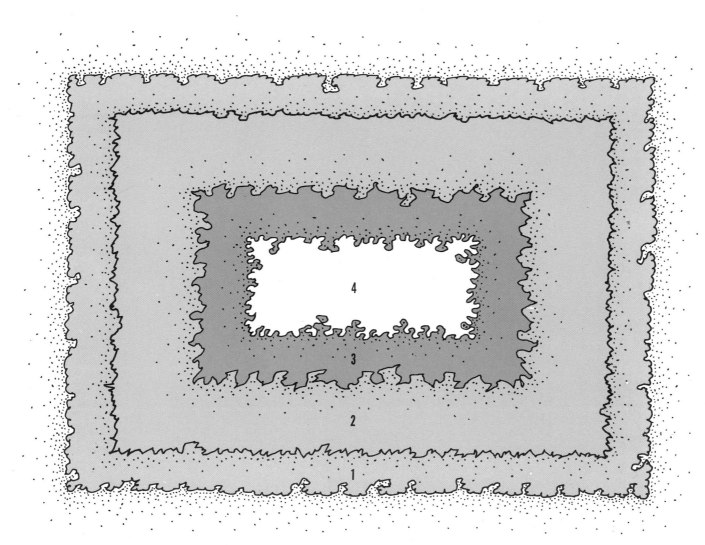

A. M. Georgens

Right: This overview of the "quarry garden" at Butchart Gardens, shows how an extensive use of annuals can create a dramatic color display. *Opposite page:* A high elevation view of a lawn, paths, and planting beds at the famous Butchart Gardens, Victoria, British Columbia.

ISLAND BED; RECTANGLE

SUN

1—White: geranium *(Pelargonium hortorum)*, petunia *(Petunia x hybrida)*, allysum *(Lobularia maritima)*, or dusty miller *(Senecio cineraria)*

2—Pink: geranium *(Pelargonium hortorum)*, aster *(Callistephus chinensis)*, petunia *(Petunia x hybrida)*, zinnia *(Zinnia elegans)*, statice *(Limonium sinuatum)*, phlox *(Phlox drummondii)*, or dianthus *(Dianthus chinensis)*

3—Lavender: petunia *(Petunia x hybrida)*, aster *(Callistephus chinensis)*, statice *(Limonium sinuatum)*, ageratum *(Ageratum houstonianum)*, candytuft *(Iberis umbellata)*, or ornamental kale *(Brassica oleracea)*

SHADE

1—White: impatiens *(Impatiens wallerana)* geranium *(Pellargonium x hortorum)*, or wax begonia *(Begonia sempervirens)*

2—Pink: impatiens (soft and hot pink can be interplanted) *(Impatiens wallerana)* wax begonia *(Begonia x semperflorens)*, nicotiana *(Nicotiana alata)*

3—Lavender: impatiens *(Impatiens wallerana)*

Left: Cheerful pink petunias and ornamental fountain grass, Pennisetum setaceum, decorate a flower bed.

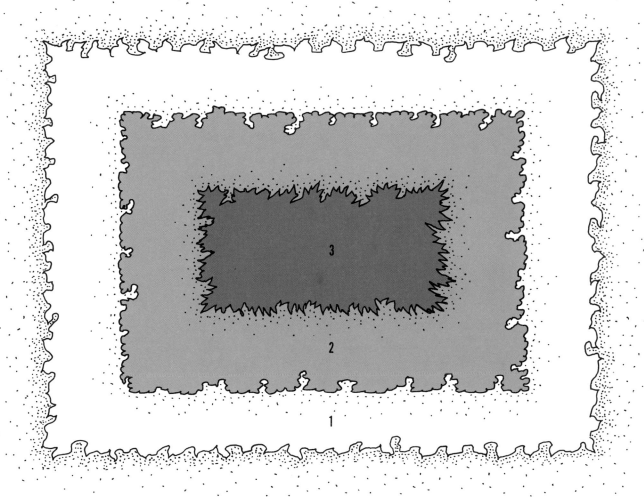

A. M. Georgens

"COLONIAL" FORMAL GARDEN; WILLIAMSBURG DESIGN

SHADE—BRIGHT COLORS

1—Orange, yellow, or scarlet mix of nasturtium
   (Trapaeolum majus)
2—Mimulus *(Mimulus* x *hybridus)* or nemesia, mixed
   colors *(Nemesia strumosa)*
3—Scarlet impatiens *(Impatiens wallerana)*

Left: A mass planting of nasturtiums decorates this California garden.

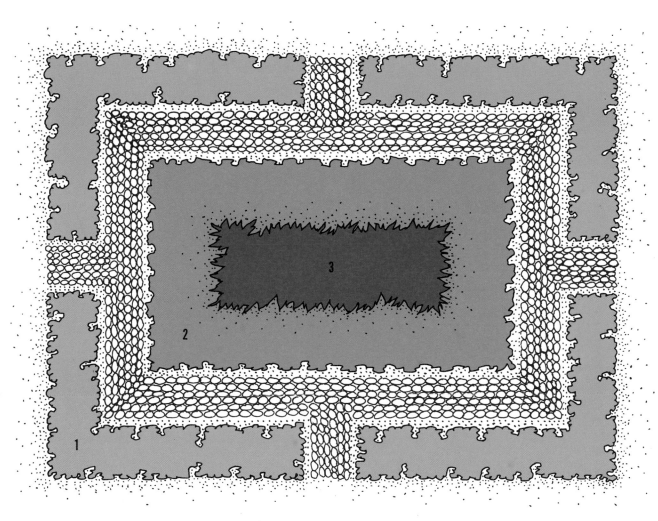

A. M. Georgens

Left: Cheerful pink petunias and ornamental fountain grass, pennisetum setaceum, decorate these flower beds.

"COLONIAL" FORMAL GARDEN; WILLIAMSBURG DESIGN

SHADE—SOFT COLORS

1—White impatiens *(Impatiens wallerana)*
2—Coral and peach impatiens *(Impatiens wallerana)*
3—Soft blue forget-me-not *(Anchusa capensis)* or white and pink nicotiana *(Nicotiana alata)*, or White foxgloves, mixed colors *(Digitalis purpurea)*
4—Optional sundial, fountain, or deeper lavender flowers: tall foxglove *(Digitalis purpurea)* or larkspur *(Consolida ambigua)*

Left: A formal garden at the headquarters of the Pennsylvania Horticultural Society in downtown Philadelphia features petunias, coleus, and portulacea in geometrically-shaped beds.

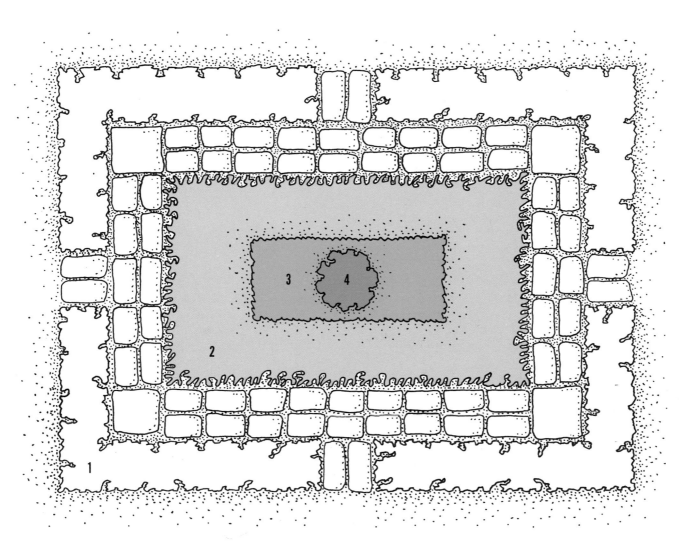

A. M. Georgens

"COLONIAL" FORMAL GARDEN; WILLIAMSBURG DESIGN

SUN—SOFT COLORS FOR CUTTING

1—White cosmos *(Cosmos bipinnatus)*
2—Pink asters *(Callistephus chinensis)*
3—Pink cockscomb *(Celosia cristata)* or pink stock *(Matthiola incana)*
4—Pink phlox *(Phlox drummondii)*
5—Pink snapdragon *(Antirrhinum majus)*
6—Yellow snapdragon *(Antirrhinum majus)*
7—Yellow hollyhocks *(Alcea rosea)*
8—Lemon yellow American marigold *(Tagetes erecta)*
9—Bright yellow zinnia *(Zinnia angustifolia)* or dahlia *(Dalia* x *hybrida)*
Path: pink pea gravel path
Option: If you want to border in yellow, use marigolds *(Tagetes erecta)*

SUN—BRIGHT COLORS FOR CUTTING

1—Hot pink cosmos *(Cosmos bipinnatus)* interplanted with gold helianthus *(Helianthus annuus)*
2—Deep lavender asters *(Callistephus chinensis)*
 —Hot pink phlox *(Phlox drummondii)*
4—Deep lavender asters *(Callistephus chinensis)*
5—Blue salvia *(Salvia farinacea)*
6—Pink snapdragons *(Antirrhinum majus)* or asters *(Callistephus chinensis)*
7—Pink cockscomb *(Celosia cristata)*
8—Lavender stock *(Matthiola incana)* or snapdragons *(Antirrhinum majus)*

Left: Zinnias and marigolds make a good companion planting in a flower bed.

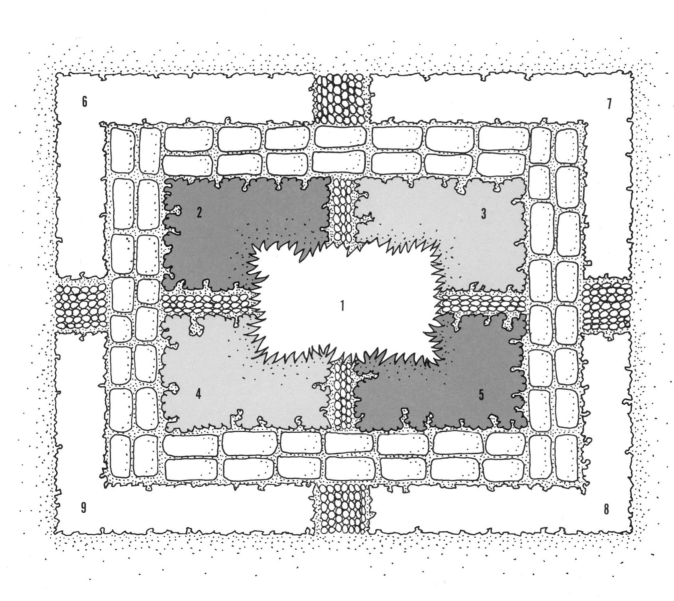

A. M. Georgens

Right: A beautiful late summer border of annuals at Stan Hywet Hall, Akron, Ohio features white cleome, scarlet sage, red and white wax begonias, silvery dusty miller, plus crimson cannas (a tropical bulb).

Opposite page: This water garden has pond margins planted with bright flowering annuals.

"FRENCH" FORMAL GARDEN; DIAMOND DESIGN

SUN—HOT COLORS FOR CUTTING

1—Pink cosmos *(Cosmos bipinnatus)*
2—Red salvia *(Salvia splendens)* or red zinnia *(Zinnia elegans)*
3—Mexican sunflowers *(Tithonia rotundifolia)* or orange marigolds *(Tagetes erecta)*
4—Blue salvia *(Salvia farinacea)* and/or cornflowers *(Centaurea cyanus)*
5—Lemon yellow marigolds *(Targetes patula)* or gold strawflowers *(Helichrysum bracteatum)*

SUN—SOFT COLORS

1—Soft pink or peach phlox *(Phlox drummondii)*
2—Blue salvia *(Salvia farinacea)*
3—Blue delphinium *(Delphinium elatum)*, scabiosa *(Scabiosa atropurpurea)*, or cornflowers *(Centaurea cyanus)*
4—Pink ornamental kale *(Brassica oleracea)* or asters *(Callistephus chinensis)*
5—Pink snapdragon *(Antirrhinum majus)* or pale pink zinnias *(Zinnia elegans)* or pink nicotiana *(Nicotiana alata)*

Left: Scarlet sage rings a pine tree at Cantigny Museum, near Chicago. The circular bed is rimmed with wax begonias.

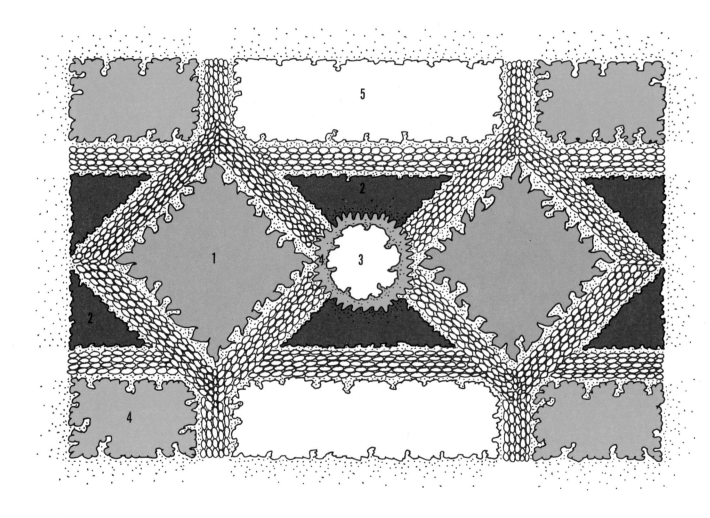

A. M. Georgens

"FRENCH" FORMAL GARDEN; DIAMOND DESIGN

SHADE—BRIGHT COLORS

1—Hot pink impatiens *(Impatiens wallerana)*
2—White impatiens *(Impatiens wallerana)*
3—Tall, powder blue ageratum *(Ageratum houstonianum)*
4—Crystal Palace lobelia *(Lobelia erinus)*
5—Lavender or crimson impatiens *(Impatiens wallerana)*

SHADE—SOFT COLORS

1—White impatiens *(Impatiens wallerana)*
2—Coral impatiens *(Impatiens wallerana)*
3—Blue salvia *(Salvia farinacea)* or Chinese forget-me-not *(Cynoglossum amabile)*
4—Pink w/white edge fibrous begonias (green foliage) *(Begonia x semperflorens)*
5—Cambridge blue lobelia *(Lobelia erinus)* or soft lavender impatiens *(Impatiens wallerana)* pink and gray

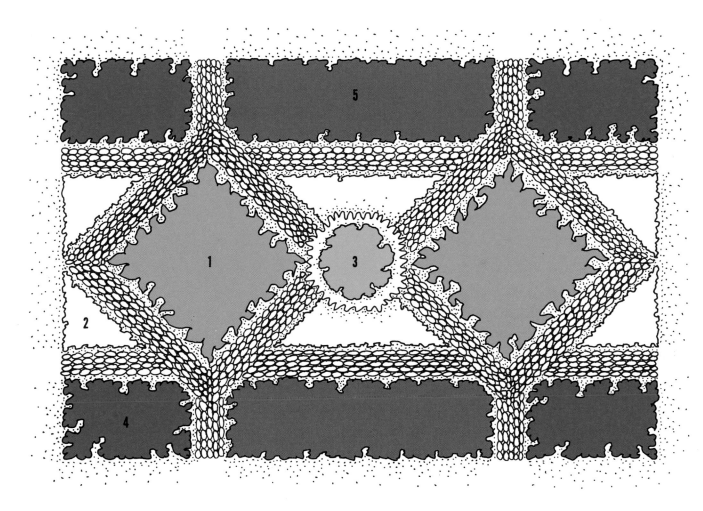

A. M. Georgens

Opposite page: A formal garden of hybrid petunias at Cantigny Museum; the center bed features 'Orchid Daddy.'
Left: Another view of the annual display garden at Cantigny Museum, using mostly zinnias, petunias, and marigolds.

"ENGLISH" FORMAL GARDEN; CARTWHEEL DESIGN

SUN—COLOR WHEEL CUTTING GARDEN

1—Red snapdragons *(Antirrhinum majus)* or red phlox *(Phlox drummondii)*, zinnia *(Zinnia elegans)*, or cockscomb *(Celosia cristata)*
2—Orange American marigolds *(Tagetes erecta)* or Mexican sunflowers *(Tithonia rotundifolia)*
3—Gold helianthum *(Helianthum annuus)*, coreopsis *(Coreopsis tinctoria)*, or gloriosa daisies *(Rudbeckia hirta burpeeii)*
4—Lemon yellow snapdragon *(Antirrhinum majus)* or marigolds *(Tagetes erecta)*
5—Blue cornflowers *(Centaurea cyanus)*
6—Purple or violet aster *(Callistephus chinensis)*, stock *(Matthiola incana)*, or snapdragon *(Anthirrhinum majus)*
7—Hot pink cosmos *(Cosmos bipinnatus)*

SUN—SOFT, COLORS FOR A CUTTING GARDEN

1—Pink stock *(Matthiola incana)*
2—Pink snapdragons *(Antirrhinum majus)*
3—Pink zinnias *(Zinnia elegans)*
4—Pink phlox *(Phlox drummondii)* or pink cosmos *(Cosmos bipinnatus)*
5—Dusty miller *(Senecia cineraria)*
6—Lavender larkspur *(Consolida ambigua)*
7—White cosmos *(Cosmos bipinnatus)* and blue delphinium *(Delphinium elatum)* or cornflowers *(Centaurea cyanus)*

Left: Dwarf hybrid zinnias make spectacular bedding plants. This variety is 'Border Beauty Rose.'

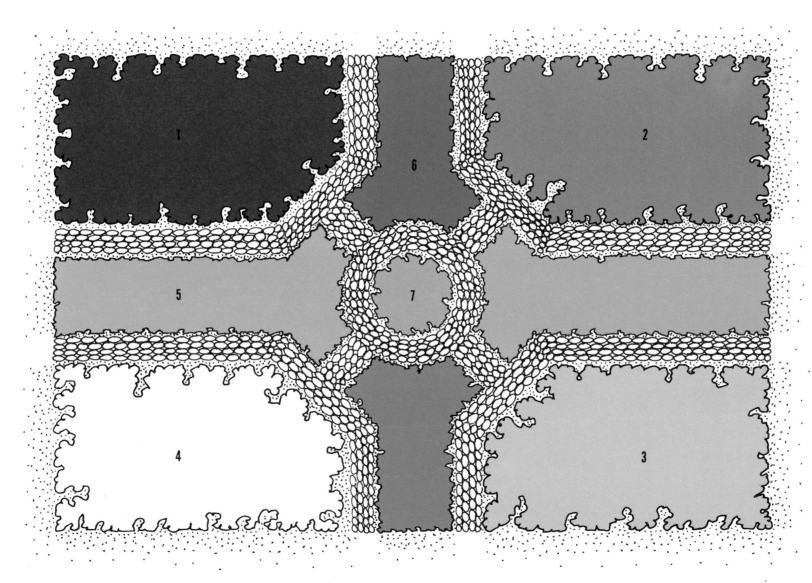

A. M. Georgens

"ENGLISH" FORMAL DESIGN; CARTWHEEL DESIGN

SHADE—SOFT COLORS

1—Peach or salmon impatiens *(Impatiens wallerana)*
2—Soft pink or rose impatiens *(Impatiens wallerana)*
3—Lavender impatiens *(Impatiens wallerana)*
4—Cambridge blue lobelia *(Lobelia erinus)*
5—White impatiens *(Impatiens wallerana)*
6—path

SHADE—WARM, SUNNY COLORS

1—Red impatiens *(Impatiens wallerana)*
2—Scarlet impatiens *(Impatiens wallerana)*
3—Yellow and orange mimulus *(Mimulus* x *hybridus)*
4—Yellow coleus *(Coleus* x *hybrida)*
5—Gray gravel path

Left: Beds filled with impatiens radiate from a circular pool, with brick paths accentuating its "cartwheel" design.

A. M. Georgens

BUTTERFLY GARDEN (TO ATTRACT BUTTERFLIES)

1—Lavender stock *(Matthiola incana)*
2—Pink stock *(Matthiola incana)*
3—Hollyhocks, mixed colors *(Alcea rosea)*
4—Scabiosa, mixed colors *(Scabiosa atropurpurea)*
5—White alyssum *(Lobularia maritima)*
6—Rose asters *(Callistephus chinensis)*
7—Lavender verbena *(Verbena x hybrida)*
8—Yellow American marigolds *(Tagetes erecta)*
9—Red zinnias *(Zinnia elegans)*
10—Strawflowers, mixed colors *(Helichrysum bracteatum)*
11—Coreopsis *(Coreopsis tinctoria)*
12—Hot pink cosmos *(Cosmos bipinnatus)*
13—Lavender asters *(Callistephus chinensis)*
Stone paths with lavender and white alyssum growing in between stones.

Left: An informal cutting garden planted with cosmos, zinnias, and celosia.

A. M. Georgens

Right: A window decorated with morning glory 'Heavenly Blue.'

CHAPTER FOUR

PLANT SELECTION GUIDE

ANNUALS ARE AN EXTREMELY VERSATILE group of plants, some low-growing and suitable for creating flowering ground covers; others tall and spire-like for sensational backgrounds. There are annuals for sun and shade, dry and moist soils, plus many other uses and conditions.

ANNUALS WITH BLUE TO PURPLE FLOWERS

Ageratum houstonianum (Flossflower)
Anchusa capensis (Cape forget-me-not)
Browallia speciosa (Amtheyst flower)
Callistephus chinensis (China aster)
Campanula medium (Canterbury bells)
Centaurea cyanus (Bachelor's button)
Consolida ambigua (Rocket larkspur)
Convolvulus tricolor (Dwarf morning glory)
Cynoglossum amabile (Chinese forget-me-not)
Gomphrena globosa (Globe amaranth)
Heliotropium arborescens (Heliotrope)
Ipomoea tricolor (Morning glory vine)
Lathyrus odoratus (Sweet pea)
Limonium sinuatum (Sea lavender)
Lisianthus russulanus (Prairie gentian)
Lobelia erinus (Edging lobelia)
Myosotis sylvatica (Forget-me-not)
Nemophila menziesii (Baby-blue eyes)

Nierembergia hippomanica (Cup flower)
Nigella damascena (Love-in-a mist)
Petunia x *hybrida* (Petunia)
Phlox drummondii (Annual phlox)
Salpiglossis sinuata (Painted tongue)
Salvia splendens (Scarlet sage)
Salvia farinacea (Blue sage)
Scabiosa atropurpurea (Pincushion flower)
Torenia fournieri (Wishbone flower)
Trachymene coerulea (Blue lace flower)
Verbena x *hybrida* (Garden verbena)
Viola x *wittrockiana* (Pansy)

ANNUALS WITH RED TO PINK FLOWERS

Amaranthus tricolor (Joseph's coat)
Alcea rosea (Hollyhock)
Antirrhinum majus (Snapdragon)
Begonia x *semperflorens* (Wax begonia)
Callistephus chinensis (China aster)
Capsicum annuum (Ornamental pepper)
Catharanthus roseus (Vinca, Periwinkle)
Celosia cristata (Cockscomb)
Clarkia hybrids (Godetia)
Cleome hasslerana (Spider flower)
Coleus x *hybridus* (Coleus)
Consolida ambigua (Larkspur)
Cosmos bipinnatus (Mexican aster)
Cuphea ignea (Firecracker plant, cigar plant)
Dahlia hybrids (Dahlia)
Dianthus species (China pink)
Digitalis purpurea (Foxglove)
Dimorphotheca sinuata (Cape marigold)
Eschscholzia californica (California poppy)
Gaillardia pulchella (Blanket flower)
Gazania rigens (Gazania)
Gerbera jamesonii (Transvaal daisy)
Gypsophila elegans (Baby's-breath)
Helichrysum bracteatum (Strawflower)
Hibiscus moscheutos (Swamp mallow)
Iberis species (Candytuft)
Impatiens species (Balsam, Patience plant)
Ipomoea x *multifida* (Cardinal climber)
Ipomoea quamoclit (Cypress vine)
Lathyrus odoratus (Sweet pea)
Lavatera hybrids (Tree mallow)
Linaria maroccana (Toadflax)
Lisianthus russulanus (Prairie gentian)
Matthiola incana (Stock)
Mimulus x *hybridus* (Monkey flower)
Nemesia strumosa (Nemesia)
Nicotiana alata (Flowering tobacco)
Nigella damascena (Love-in-a-mist)
Papaver species (Iceland poppy, Shirley poppy)
Pelargonium x *hortorum* (Geranium)
Petunia x *hybrida* (Petunia)

Phlox drummondii (Annual phlox)
Portulaca grandiflora (Rose moss)
Salpiglossis sinuata (Painted tongue)
Salvia splendens (Scarlet sage)
Scabiosa atropurpurea (Pincushion flower)
Schizanthus x *wisetonesis* (Butterfly flower)
Tropaeolum majus (Nasturtium)
Verbena x *hybrida* (Garden verbena)
Viola x *wittrockiana* (Pansy)
Xeranthemum annuum (Immortelle)
Zinnia elegans (Zinnia)

ANNUALS WITH GREEN FLOWERS

Coleus hybrids (variety, Saber Lime Green)
Moluccella laevis (Bells-of-Ireland)
Nicotiana alata (variety, Limelight)
Zinnia elegans (variety, Envy)

ANNUALS WITH BLACK OR BROWN FLOWERS

Viola x *wittrockiana* (Pansy variety, Jet Black)
Salpiglossis sinuata (Velvet flower,

Red salvia and impatiens decorate a slope at Leaming's Run Garden, near Cape May, New Jersey.

ANNUALS WITH YELLOW AND ORANGE FLOWERS

Alcea rosea (Hollyhock)
Calendula officinalis (Pot marigold)
Celosia cristata (Cockscomb)
Coreopsis tinctoria (Calliopsis)
Cosmos sulphureus (Orange cosmos)
Dahlia hybrids (Dahlia)
Dimorphotheca sinuata (Cape marigold)
Dyssodia tenuiloba (Dahlberg daisy)
Eschscholzia californica (California poppy)
Gaillardia pulchella (Blanket flower)
Gazania rigens (Gazania)
Gerbera jamesonii (Transvaal daisy)
Gomphrena globosa (Globe amaranth)
Helianthus species (Sunflower)
Linaria maroccana (Toadflax)
Matthiola incana (Stock)
Mimulus x *hybridus* (Monkey flower)
Nemesia strumosa (Nemesia)
Papaver nudicaule (Iceland poppy)
Pelargonium x *hortorum* (Geranium)
Portulaca grandiflora (Rose moss)
Rudbeckia hirta (Gloriosa daisy)
Sanvitalia procumbens (Creeping zinnia)
Tagetes species (Marigolds)
Thunbergia alata (Black-eyed Susan vine)
Tithonia rotundifolia (Mexican sunflower)
Tropaeolum majus (Nasturtium)
Vendium fastuosum (Monarch-of-the-veldt)
Verbena x *hybrida* (Garden verbena)
Viola x *wittrockiana* (Pansy)
Zinnia species (Zinnia)

ANNUALS WITH WHITE FLOWERS

Ageratum houstonianum (Flossflower)
Alcea rosea (Hollyhock)
Antirrhinum majus (Snapdragon)
Arctotis stoechadifolia (African daisy)
Begonia x *semperflorens* (Wax begonia)
Callistephus chinensis (China aster)
Catharanthrus roseus (Madagascar periwinkle)
Cleome hasslerana (Spider flower)
Dahlia hybrid (Dahlia)
Dianthus species (China pink)
Dimorphotheca sinuata (Cape marigold)
Eschscholzia californica (California poppy)
Gerbera jamesonii (Transvaal daisy)
Gypsophila elegans (Baby's-breath)
Helichrysum bracteatum (Strawflower)

Iberis species (Candytuft)
Impatiens balsamina (Balsam)
Impatiens wallerana (Patience plant)
Ipomoea alba (Moonflower vine)
Lathyrus odoratus (Sweet pea)
Lobelia erinus (Edging lobelia)
Lobularia maritima (Sweet alyssum)
Matthiola incana (Stock)
Nicotiana alata (Flowering tobacco)
Papaver species (Iceland poppy, Shirley poppy)
Pelargonium x *hortorum* (Geranium)
Petunia x *hybrida* (Petunia)
Phlox drummondii (Annual phlox)
Salvia splendens (Scarlet sage)
Scabiosa atropurpurea (Pincushion flower)
Thunbergia alata (Black-eyed Susan vine)
Verbena x *hybrida* (Garden verbena)
Viola x *wittrockiana* (Pansy)

Opposite page: A large formal bed featuring mostly petunias, marigolds, and dusty miller is planted to form a huge star design.
Left: White vinca makes a good companion in a border.

LOW-GROWING ANNUALS

Ageratum houstonianum (Flossflower)
Antirrhinum majus, dwarf cultivars (Snapdragon)
Arctotis (African daisy)
Begonia x *semperflorens* (Wax begonia)
Calendula officinalis (Pot marigold)
Capsicum annuum (Ornamental pepper)
Catharanthus roseus (Madagascar periwinkle)
Celosia cristata (Cockscomb)
Coleus x *hybridus* (Coleus)
Cuphea ignea (Firecracker plant, Cigar plant)
Dahlia hybrids (Dahlia)
Dimorphotheca sinuata (Cape marigold)
Dyssodia tenuiloba (Dahlberg daisy)
Gaillardia pulchella (Blanket flower)
Gazania rigens (Gazania)
Gerbera jamesonii (Transvaal daisy)
Iberis species (Candytuft)
Impatiens wallerana (Patience plant)
Limnanthes douglasii (Meadow foam)
Linaria maroccana (Toadflax)
Lobelia erinus (Edging lobelia)
Lobularia maritima (Sweet alyssum)
Myosotis sylvatica (Forget-me-not)
Nemesia strumosa (Nemesia)
Nemophila menziesii (Baby-blue eyes)
Nicotiana alata (Flowering tobacco)
Nierembergia hippomanica (Cup flower)
Pelargonium x *hortorum* (Geranium)
Petunia x *hybrida* (Petunia)
Phlox drummondii (Annual phlox)
Portulaca grandiflora (Rose moss)
Salvia species (Sage)
Sanvitalia procumbens (Creeping zinnia)
Schizanthus x *wisetonensis* (Butterfly flower)
Senecio cineraria (Dusty miller)
Tagetes species (Marigolds)
Tropaeolum majus (Nasturtium)
Verbena x *hybrida* (Garden verbena)
Viola x *wittrockiana* (Pansy)
Zinnia species (Zinnia)

MEDIUM-GROWING ANNUALS

Anchusa capensis (Cape forget-me-not)
Amaranthus tricolor (Joseph's coat)
Calendula officinalis (Pot marigold)
Callistephus chinensis (China aster)
Catharanthus roseus (Madagascar periwinkle)
Clarkia hybrids (Godetia)
Cleome hasslerana (Spider flower)
Coleus x *hybridus* (Coleus)
Dahlia hybrids (Dahlia)
Dianthus barbatus (Sweet William)
Eschscholzia californica (California poppy)
Euphorbia marginata (Snow-on-the-mountain)
Gomphrena globosa (Globe amaranth)
Helianthus species, dwarf cultivars (Sunflowers)
Helichrysum bracteatum (Strawflower)
Heliotropium arborescens (Heliotrope)
Impatiens wallerana (Patience plant)
Kochia scoparia (Burning bush)
Lavatera hybrids (Tree mallow)
Limonium species (Algerian sea lavender, statice)
Mirabilis jalapa (Four-o'clock)
Pelargonium x *hortorum* (Geranium)
Petunia x *hybrida* (Petunia)
Papaver species (Poppies)
Rudbeckia hirta (Gloriosa daisy)
Schizanthus x *wisetonensis* (Butterfly flower)
Tagetes species (Marigolds)
Zinnia elegans (Zinnia)

TALL-GROWING ANNUALS

Alcea rosea (Hollyhock)
Amaranthus tricolor (Joseph's coat)
Antirrhinum majus (Tall snapdragon)
Campanula media (Canterbury bell)
Celosia cristata (Plumed cockscomb)
Cleome hasslerana (Spider flower)
Consolida ambigua (Rocket larkspur)
Cosmos bipinnatus (Cosmos)
Delphinium elatum (Delphinium)
Digitalis purpurea (Foxglove)
Helianthus species (Sunflower)
Hibiscus moscheutos (Swamp mallow)
Tithonia rotundifolia (Mexican sunflower)
Zea mays var. *japonica* (Ornamental corn)
Zinnia elegans, tallest cultivars (Zinnia)

HEAT-TOLERANT ANNUALS

Amaranthus tricolor (Joseph's coat)
Begonia x *semperflorens-cultorum* (Wax begonia)
Capsicum annuum (Ornamental pepper)
Catharanthus roseus (Madagascar periwinkle)
Celosia cristata (Cockscomb)
Convolvulus tricolor (Dwarf morning glory)
Coreopsis tinctoria (Calliopsis)
Cuphea ignea (Firecracker plant, cigar plant)
Dahlia hybrids (Dahlia)
Dyssodia tenuiloba (Dahlberg daisy)
Euphorbia marginata (Snow-on-the-mountain)
Gomphrena globosa (Globe amaranth)
Helianthus species (Sunflowers)
Kochia scoparia (Burning bush)
Mirabilis jalapa (Four-o'clock)
Petunia x *hybrida* (Petunia)
Portulaca grandiflora (Rose moss)
Rudbeckia hirta (Gloriosa daisy)
Salvia species (Sage)
Sanvitalia procumbens (Creeping zinnia)
Senecio cineraria (Dusty miller)
Tagetes species (Marigold)
Tithonia rotundifolia (Mexican sunflower)
Verbena x *hybrida* (Garden verbena)
Zinnia species (Zinnia)

ANNUALS FOR MOIST SOIL

Cleome hasslerana (Spider-flower)
Euphorbia marginata (Snow-on-the-mountain)
Hibiscus moscheutos (Swamp mallow)
Limnanthes douglasii (Meadow foam)
Mimulus x *hybridus* (Monkey flower)
Myosotis sylvatica (Forget-me-not)
Primula species (Primrose)
Senecio x *hybridus* (Cineraria)
Torenia fournieri (Wishbone flower)
Tropaeolum majus (Nasturtium)
Viola x *wittrockiana* (Pansy)

ANNUALS FOR SHADE

Begonia x *semperflorens* (Wax begonia)
Browallia speciosa (Amethyst flower)
Campanula medium (Canterbury bells)
Coleus x *hybridus* (Coleus)
Impatiens wallerana (Patience plant)
Mimulus x *hybridus* (Monkey flower)
Myosotis sylvatica (Forget-me-not)
Nemophilia menziesii (Baby-blue eyes)
Nicotiana alata (Flowering tobacco)
Primula species (Primrose)
Senecio x *hybridus* (Cineraria)
Thunbergia alata (Black-eyed Susan vine)
Torenia fournieri (Wishbone flower)
Viola x *wittrockiana* (Pansy)

ANNUALS FOR INDOORS

Begonia x *semperflorens* (Wax begonia)
Browallia speciosa (Amethyst flower)
Capsicum annuum (Ornamental pepper)
Catharanthus roseus (Madagascar periwinkle)
Coleus x *hybridus* (Coleus)
Cuphea ignea (Firecracker plant, Cigar plant)
Heliotropium arborescens (Heliotrope)
Impatiens wallerana (Patience plant)
Nierembergia hippomanica (Cup flower)
Pelargonium x *hortorum* (Geranium)
Thunbergia alata (Black-eyed Susan vine)
Torenia fournieri (Wishbone flower)

Above left: A bed featuring snapdragons (antirrhinums) and coleus; the snapdragons are lighted by morning sun, the coleus can be seen in the shade of a tree.
Below left: The gloriosa daisy, 'Pinwheel.'

Opposite page: A mixed bed of annuals featuring blue salvia, yellow American marigolds, purple petunias, and red coleus.

ANNUALS FOR CUTTING

*Asterisked varieties make good everlastings.

Antirrhinum majis (Snapdragon)
Calendula officinalis (Pot marigold)
Callistephus chinensis (China aster)
Celosia cristata (Cockscomb)
Centaurea cyanus (Cornflower)
Chrysanthemum carinatum (Painted daisy)
Consolida ambigua (Larkspur)
Cosmos bipinnatus (Cosmos)
Dahlia x *hybrida* (Dahlia)
Delphinium elatum (Delphinium)
Dianthus caryophyllus (Carnation)
Digitalis purpurea (Foxglove)
Gaillardia pulchella (Gayflower)
*_Gomphrena globosa_ (Globe flower)
Gypsophila elegans (Baby's-breath)
Helianthus annuus (Sunflower)
*_Helichrysum bracteatum_ (Strawflower)
Lathyrus odoratus (Sweet pea)
*_Limonium sinuatum_ (Statice)
Lisianthus russulanus (Prairie gentian)
Matthiola incana (Stocks)
*_Molucella laevis_ (Bells of Ireland)
Papaver nudicaule (Iceland poppy)
Penstemon gloxiniodes (Beard tongue)
Rudbeckia hirta (Gloriosa daisy)
Salvia farinacea (Blue salvia)
Scabiosa atropurpurea (Sweet scabious)
Tagetes erecta (American marigold)
Venidium fastuosum (Monarch-of-the-veldt)
*_Xeranthemum annuum_ (Immortelle)
Zinnia elegans (Zinnia)

ANNUALS THAT NATURALIZE

Alcea rosea (Hollyhock)
Anchusa capensis (Cape forget-me-not)
Calendula officinalis (Pot marigold)
Centaurea cyanus (Cornflower)
Coreopsis tinctoria (Calliopsis)
Cosmos bipinnatus (Cosmos)
Cosmos sulphureus (Orange cosmos)
Cynoglossum amabile (Chinese forget-me-not)
Dianthus chinensis (China pink)
Dyssodia tenuiloba (Dahlberg daisy)
Eschscholzia californica (California poppy)
Euphorbia marginata (Snow-on-the-mountain)
Limnanthes douglasii (Meadow foam)
Linaria maroccana (Toadflax)
Lobularia maritima (Sweet alyssum)
Mirabilis jalapa (Four-o'clock)
Moluccella laevis (Bells of Ireland)
Myosotis sylvatica (Forget-me-not)
Nigella damascena (Love-in-a-mist)
Papaver nudicaule (Iceland poppy)
Papaver rhoeas (Shirley poppy)
Portulaca grandiflora (Rose moss)
Rudbeckia hirta (Gloriosa daisy)

ANNUALS WITH DECORATIVE FOLIAGE

Amaranthus caudatus (Love-lies-bleeding)
Amaranthus tricolor (Joseph's coat)
Begonia x *semperflorens* (Wax begonia)
Brassica olereacea (Ornamental cabbage, flowering kale)
Coleux x *hybridus* (Coleus)
Euphorbia marginata (Snow-on-the-mountain)
Ipomoea species (Morning glory)
Kochia scoparia (Burning bush)
Pelargonium x *hortorum* (Geranium)
Senecio cineraria (Dusty miller)
Tagetes 'Irish Lace' (Irish lace marigold)
Zea mays var. *japonica* (Ornamental corn)

ANNUALS FOR EDGING

Ageratum houstonianum (Floss flower)
Antirrhinum majus (Snapdragon)
Begonia x *semperflorens* (Wax begonia)
Brassica olereacea (Ornamental kale)
Browallia speciosa (Amethyst flower)
Callistephus chinensis (China aster)
Capsicum annuum (Ornamental pepper)
Celosia plumosa (Cockscomb)
Cuphea ignea (Firecracker plant, cigar plant)
Dianthus chinensis (China pink)
Iberis species (Candytuff)
Impatiens wallerana (Patience plant)
Linaria maroccana (Toadflax)
Lobelia erinus (Edging lobelia)
Nierembergia hippomanica (Cup flower)
Petunia x *hybrida* (Petunia)
Phlox drummondii (Annual phlox)
Portulaca grandiflora (Rose moss)
Senecio cineraria (Dusty miller)
Tagetes signata (Signet marigold)
Tagetes patula (French marigold)
Torenia fournieri (Wishbone flower)
Viola x *wittrockiana* (Pansy)
Zinnia, dwarf cultivars (Zinnia)

ANNUALS FOR FRAGRANCE

Cheiranthus cheiri (Wallflower)
Dianthus barbatus (Sweet William)
Dianthus caryophyllus (Carnation)
Heliotropium arborescens (Heliotrope)
Lathyrus odoratus (Sweet pea)
Lobularia maritima (Sweet alyssum)
Matthiola incana (Stock)
Mirabilis jalapa (Four-o'clock)
Nicotiana alata (Flowering tobacco)
Petunia x *hybrida* (Petunia)
Reseda odorata (Mignonette)
Scabiosa atropurpurea (Sweet scabious)

ANNUALS FOR HANGING BASKETS

Browallia speciosa (Amethyst flower)
Coleus x *hybrida* (Coleus)
Impatiens wallerana (Patience plant)
Lobelia erinus (Edging lobelia)
Lobularia maritima (Sweet alyssum)
Nemesia strumosa (Nemesia)
Pelargonium x *hortorum* (Geranium)
Petunia x *hybrida* (Petunia)
Sanvitalia procumbens (Creeping zinnia)
Schizanthus x *wisetonensis* (Butterly flower)
Thunbergia alata (Black-eyed Susan vine)
Tropaeolum majus (Nasturtium)
Verbena x *hybrida* (Garden verbena)
Viola x *wittrockiana* (Pansy)

VINING ANNUALS

Cobaea scandens (Cup and saucer vine)
Cucurbita pepo (Gourds)
Dolichos lablab (Hyacinth bean)
Ipomoea alba (Moonflower vine)
Ipomoea x *multifida* (Cardinal climber)
Ipomoea nil, I. purpurea, I. tricolor (Morning glory vine)
Ipomoea quamoclit (Cypress vine)
Lathyrus odoratus (Sweet pea)
Thunbergia alata (Black-eyed Susan vine)
Tropaeolum majus (Nasturtium) if trained

Opposite page: This color border features a mixtures of giant-flowered zinnias against an evergreen hedge.

ANNUAL FLOWERING GUIDE

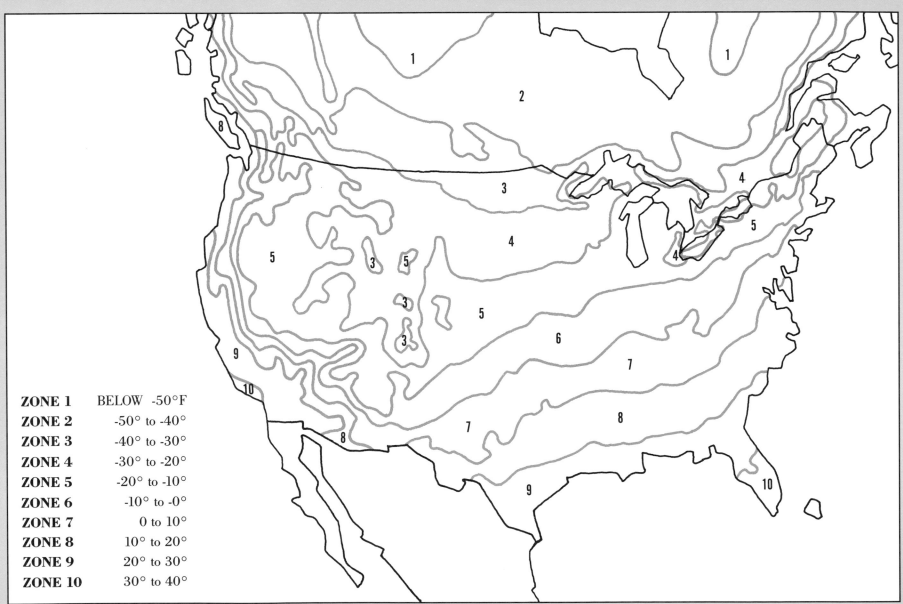

ZONE 1	BELOW -50°F
ZONE 2	-50° to -40°
ZONE 3	-40° to -30°
ZONE 4	-30° to -20°
ZONE 5	-20° to -10°
ZONE 6	-10° to -0°
ZONE 7	0 to 10°
ZONE 8	10° to 20°
ZONE 9	20° to 30°
ZONE 10	30° to 40°

ANNUAL FLOWERING GUIDE

	January	February	March	April	May	June	July	August	September	October	November	December
Ageratum houstonianum (Floss flower)						■	■	■	■			
Alcea rosea (Hollyhock)							■	■				
Amaranthus tricolor (Josephs-coat)						■						
Anchusa capensis (Summer Forget-me-not)						■						
Antirrhinum majus (Snapdragon)									■			
Arctotis stoechadifolia (African Daisy)						■						
Begonia semperflorens (Wax Begonia)						■	■	■	■			
Brachycome iberidifolia (Swan River Daisy)						■						
Brassica oleracea (Ornamental Kale)										■	■	■
Browallia speciosa (Lovely Browalia)							■	■	■			
Calendula officinalis (Pot-Marigold)					■				■			
Callistephus chinensis (China Aster)								■				
Capsicum annuum (Ornamental Pepper)							■	■	■			
Catharanthus roseus (Vinca, Periwinkle)						■	■	■	■			
Celosia cristata (Crested Cockscomb)							■					
Centaurea cyanus (Cornflower)						■						
Chrysanthemum carinatum (Painted Daisy)							■					
Clarkia amoena (Godetia, Satin Flower)						■						
Cleome hasslerana (Spiderflower)							■	■	■	■		
Cobaea scandens (Cup-and-saucer Vine)								■	■			
Coleus x *hybrida* (Flame Nettle)					■	■			■	■		
Consolida ambigua (Larkspur)						■						
Coreopsis tinctoria (Plains Coreopsis)						■						

	January	February	March	April	May	June	July	August	September	October	November	December
Cosmos bipinnatus (Cosmos)						▓	▓	▓	▓	▓		
Cucurbita pepo (Ornamental Gourds)							▓	▓	▓			
Cynoglossum amabile (Chinese Forget-me-not)						▓	▓	▓				
Dahlia x *hybrida* (Bedding Dahlias)						▓	▓	▓	▓	▓		
Datura metel (Angel's Trumpet)						▓	▓	▓	▓			
Delphinium elatum (Candle Larkspur)						▓						
Dianthus caryophyllus (Carnation)							▓	▓	▓			
Dianthus chinensis (Dianthus)					▓	▓						
Digitalis purpurea (Foxglove)						▓	▓					
Dimorphotheca sinuata (Cape Marigold, African Daisy)												
Dorotheanus bellidiformis (Livingstone Daisy)												
Eschscholzia californica (California-poppy)					▓							
Euphorbia marginata (Snow-on-the-Mountain)							▓	▓				
Gaillardia pulchella (Blanket Flower)						▓	▓	▓	▓			
Gazania ringens (Rainbow Daisy)						▓	▓	▓				
Gomphrena globusa (Globe Amaranth)							▓	▓	▓	▓		
Gypsophila elegans (Baby's-breath)						▓	▓					
Helianthus annuus (Sunflower)												
Helichrysum bracteatum (Straw-flower)							▓	▓	▓			
Hibiscus moscheutos (Southern Hibiscus)												
Hunnemannia fumariifolia (Mexican Tulip Poppy)						▓						
Iberis umbellata (Candytuft)					▓	▓						
Impatiens balsamina (Balsam)						▓	▓	▓	▓			

	January	February	March	April	May	June	July	August	September	October	November	December
Impatiens wallerana (Patience-plant)					■	■	■	■	■	■		
Ipomoea alba (Moonflower)							■	■	■			
Ipomoea tricolor (Morning Glory)							■	■	■	■		
Kochia scoparia (Burning Bush)							■	■	■	■		
Lathyrus odoratus (Sweet Pea)							■	■				
Lavatera trimestris (Rose-mallow)							■	■				
Limnathes douglasii (Meadow-foam)					■	■						
Limonium sinuatum (Statice)							■	■				
Linaria maroccana (Toadflax)							■	■				
Lisianthus russulanus (Eustoma grandiflorum) (Prairie-gentian)							■	■	■			
Lobelia erinus (Lobelia)						■	■	■				
Lobularia maritima (Alyssum)				■	■	■	■	■	■	■		
Machaeranthera tanacetifolia (Tahoka-daisy)							■	■				
Matthiola incana (Common Stocks)							■	■	■			
Mimulus hybridus (Monkey-flower)							■					
Mirabilis jalapa (Four-O'clock)							■	■	■			
Moluccella laevis (Bells-of-Ireland)							■	■	■			
Myosotis sylvatica (Forget-me-not)					■							
Nemesia strumosa (Nemesia)							■	■	■			
Nemophilia menziensii (Baby-blue-eyes)							■					
Nicotiana alata (Flowering Tobacco)							■	■	■			
Nierembergia hippomanica (Capflower)						■	■					

		January	February	March	April	May	June	July	August	September	October	November	December
Nigella damascena	(Love-in-a-mist)							●	●	●			
Papaver nudicaule	(Iceland Poppy)					●	●	●					
Papaver rhoeas	(Shirley Poppy)					●	●						
Pelargonium x *hortorum*	(Geranium)						●	●	●	●	●		
Penstemon x *gloxinioides*	(Bearded Tongue)						●	●	●	●			
Petunia x *hybrida*	(Petunia)						●	●	●	●	●		
Phlox drummondii	(Phlox)						●	●					
Portulaca grandiflora	(Moss Rose)						●	●	●	●			
Reseda odorata	(Mignonette)						●	●	●	●			
Ricinus communis	(Castor-bean Plant)							●	●	●	●		
Rudbeckia hirta burpeeii	(Black-eyed-susan)						●	●	●	●			
Salpiglossis sinuata	(Velvet-flower)						●	●					
Salvia farinacea	(Blue Salvia)						●	●	●	●	●		
Salvia splendens	(Scarlet Sage)						●	●	●	●			
Sanvitalia procumbens	(Creeping Zinnia)						●	●	●	●			
Scabiosa atropurpurea	(Sweet Scabious)						●	●					
Schiznathus x *wisetonensis*	(Butterfly-flower)					●	●						
Senecio cineraria	(Dusty Miller)					●	●	●	●	●	●		
Tagetes erecta	(American Marigold)						●	●	●	●			
Tagetes patula	(French Marigold)						●	●	●	●			
Tagetes tenuifolia	(Striped Marigold)						●	●	●	●			
Thunbergia alata	(Black-eyed Susan Vine)							●	●	●			
Tithonia rotundifolia	(Mexican Sunflower)							●	●	●			

	January	February	March	April	May	June	July	August	September	October	November	December
Torenia fournieri (Wishbone flower)							■	■	■	■		
Tropaeolium majus (Nasturtium)						■	■	■	■	■		
Venidium fastuosum (Monarch-of-the-veldt)							■					
Verbena x hybrida (Summer Verbena)							■	■	■			
Viola tricolor (Pansy)					■	■						
Xeranthemium annuum (Immortelle)						■	■					
Zinnia angustifolia (Classic Zinnia)							■	■	■			
Zinnia elegans (Zinnia)							■	■	■			

MAIL-ORDER SOURCES OF FLOWERING ANNUAL SEEDS

Applewood Seed Co.
Box 10761, Edgemont Station
Golden, CO 80401

W. Atlee Burpee
300 Park Ave.
Warminster, PA 18974

Comstock Ferre & Co.
263 Main St.
Wethersfield, CT 06109

Dominion Seed House
115 Guelph St.
Georgetown, Ontario
Canada L7G 4A2

Henry Field Seed & Nursey Co.
407 Sycamore St.
Shenandoah, IA 51602

Gurney Seed & Nursery Co.
Yankton, SD 57079

Joseph Harris Co.
Moreton Farm
Rochester, NY 14624

H.G. Hastings Co.
Box 4274
Atlanta, GA 30302

The Charles Hart Seed Co.
Main & Hart Streets
Wethersfield, CT 06109

J. L. Hudson, Seedsman
Box 1058
Redwood City, CA 94064

Johnny's Selected Seeds
Albion, ME 04910

J.W. Jung Seed Co.
Randolph, WI 53956

Laval Seeds Inc.
3505 Boul St. Martin
Chomedey Laval
Quebec, Canda H7V 2T3

Orol Ledden & Sons
Center St.
Sewell, NJ 08080

Earl May Seed & Nursery Co.
Shenandoah, IA 51603

McLaughlins Seeds
Box 550
Mead, WA 99021

Mellingers Inc.
North Lima, OH 44452

Nichol's Herbs & Rare Seeds
1190 N. Pacific Highway
Albany, OR 97321

L. L. Olds Seed Co.
2901 Packers Ave.
Madison, WI 53707

George W. Park Seed Inc.
Greenwood, SC 29647

W. H. Perron & Co. Ltd.
515 Labelle Blvd.
Chomedey Laval
Quebec, Canada H7V 2T3

Plants of the Southwest
1812 Second Street
Santa Fe, NM 87501

Clyde Robin Seed Company
Box 2366
Castro Valley, CA 94546

Stokes Seeds Inc.
Box 548
Buffalo, NY 14240

Thompson & Morgan
Box 1308
Jackson, NJ 08527

Otis S. Twilley Seed Co.
Box 65
Trevose, PA 19047

This beautiful garden display on the campus of California Polytechnic Institute in San Luis Obispo, California features popular annuals.

INDEX OF BOTANICAL AND COMMON NAMES

A

African Daisy. *See Arctotis stoechadifolia;*
  Dimorphotheca sinuata
African Marigold. *See Tagetes erecta*
Ageratum houstonianum, 28
Alcea rosea, 28
Alyssum. *See Lobularia maritima*
Amaranth. *See Gomphrena globosa*
Amaranthus tricolor, 29
American Marigold. *See Tagetes*
  erecta
Anchusa capensis, 29
Angel's Trumpet. *See Datura metel*
Animals, 21
Annuals
  color guide, 119-23
  color range, 10
  for cutting, 128
  with decorative foliage, 128
  ease and dependability of growth, 9
  for edging, 131
  flowering guide, 132-37
  flowering time, 9
  for fragrance, 131
  for hanging baskets, 131
  heat-tolerant, 126
  height, 124-25
  for indoors, 127
  low-growing, 124
  medium growing, 124
  for moist soil, 126
  naturalizing, 128
  seeds. See Seeds
  for shade, 127
  tall-growing, 125
  vining, 131
Antirrhinum majus, 30
Arctotis stoechadifolia, 30
Aster. *See Callistephus chinensis*

B

Baby-blue-eyes. *See Nemophila*
  menziesii
Baby's-breath. *See Gypsophila*
  elegans
Bachelor's-button. *See Centaurea*
  cyanus
Balsam. *See Impatiens balsamina*
Bearded Tongue. *See Penstemon*
  gloxinioides
Bedding Dahlia. *See Dahlia hybrida*
Beds, *20–21,* 22–25
  formal, *122–23*
  rectangular island, 86–95
Begonia semperflorens, 31
Bells-of-Ireland. *See Moluccella*
  laevis
Black-eyed Susan. *See Rudbeckia*
  hirta burpeeii
Black-eyed Susan Vine. *See Thunbergia*
  alata
Blanket Flower. *See Gaillardia*
  pulchella
Blue Salvia. *See Salvia farinacea*
Borders, *12–13,* 22–25, *42, 74,*
  118–19, 123–24
Brachycome iberidifolia, 31
Brassica oleracea, 32
Browallia sp., 32
Burning Bush. *See Kochia scoparia*
Butterfly Flower. *See Schizanthus*
  wisetonensis
Butterfly gardens, 116–17

C

Cabbage. *See Brassica oleracea*
Calendula officinalis, 33
California-poppy. *See Eschscholzia*
  californica
Calliopsis. *See Coreopsis tinctoria*
Callistephus chinensis, 33
Candytuft. *See Iberis umbellata*
Cape Marigold. *See Dimorphotheca*
  sinuata
Capsicum annuum, 34
Carnation. *See Dianthus caryophyllus*
Carpet bedding, 10
Cartwheel designs, 112–15
Castor Bean Plant. *See Ricinus*
  communis
Catharanthus roseus, 34
Celosia cristata, 36
Centaurea cyanus, 36
China Aster. *See Callistephus*
  chinensis
Chinese Forget-me-not. *See*
  Cynoglossum amabile
Chrysanthemum carinatum, 37
Clarkia amoena, 37
Classic Zinnia. *See Zinnia*
  angustifolia
Cobaea scandens, 38
Cockscomb. *See Celosia cristata*
Coleus hybrida, 39
Colonial formal gardens, 96–105
Color guide, 119–23
Compost, 21
Consolida ambigua, 39
Containers, *20–21,* 21–25
Coreopsis tinctoria, 40
Cornflower. *See Centaurea cyanus*
Cosmos bipinnatus, 40
Creeping Zinnia. *See Sanvitalia*
  procumbens
Crested Cockscomb. *See Celosia*
  cristata
Cucurbita pepo, 41
Cup-and-saucer vine. *See Cobaea*
  scandens
Cupflower. *See Nierembergia*
  hippomanica

Cutting gardens, 25
   annuals for, 128
Cynoglossum amabile, 41

D

Dahlberg Daisy. *See Dyssodia
   tenuiloba*
Dahlia hybrida, 43
Daisy. *See Arctotis stoechadifolia;
   Brachycome iberidifolia;
   Chrysanthemum carinatum;
   Dimorphoteca sinuata;
   Dorotheanus bellidiformis;
   Dyssodia tenuiloba; Gazania
   ringens; Machaeranthera
   tanacetifolia*
Datura metel, 43
Decorative foliage, 128
Deer, 21
Delphinium elatum, 44
Diamond designs, 106–9
Dianthus caryophyllus, 44
Dianthus chinensis, 45
Digitalis purpurea, 45
Dimorphotheca sinuata, 46
Diseases, 21
Dorotheanus bellidiformis, 46
Dusty Miller. *See Senecio cineraria*
Dyssodia tenuiloba, 47

E

Edging, annuals for, 131
English formal gardens, 112–15
Eschscholzia californica, 47
Euphorbia marginata, 48
Eustoma grandiflorum, 60

F

Fertilizing, 19
Flame Nettle. *See Coleus hybrida*
Floss Flower. *See Ageratum
   houstonianum*
Flower color guide, 119–23
Flowering guide, 132–37
Flowering Tobacco. *See Nicotiana
   alata*
Foliage, decorative, 128
Foraging animals, 21
Forget-me-not. *See Anchusa capensis;
   Cynoglossum amabile; Myosotis
   sylvatica*
Four-o'-clock. *See Mirabilis jalapa*
Foxglove. *See Digitalis purpurea*
Foxy. *See Digitalis purpurea*
Fragrance, annuals for, 131
French formal gardens, 106–9
French Marigold. *See Tagetes patula*

G

Gaillardia pulchella, 48
Garden plans
   to attract butterflies, 116–17
   colonial formal, 96–105
   English formal, 112–15
   French formal, 106–9
   rectangular island beds, 86–95
Gazania rigens, 49
Gentian. *See Lisianthus russulanus*
Geranium. *See Pelargonium hortorum*
Giverney Garden (France), *10–11*
Globe Amaranth. *See Gomphrena
   globosa*
Gloriosa Daisy. *See Rudbeckia hirta burpeeii*
Godetia. *See Clarkia amoena*
Goldsmith Seeds (flower breeders),
   26–27
Gomphrena globosa, 49
Gourd. *See Cucurbita pepo*
Gypsophila elegans, 50

H

Hanging baskets, annuals for, 131
Hardiness zones, 132
Heat-tolerant annuals, 126
Helianthus annuus, 50
Helichrysum bracteatum, 52
Hibiscus moscheutos, 52

Hollyhock. *See Alcea rosea*
Hunnemannia fumariifolia, 53

I

Iberis umbellata, 53
Iceland Poppy. *See Papaver nudicaule*
Immortelle. *See Xeranthemum annuum*
Impatiens balsamina, 54
Impatiens wallerana, 54
Indoor annuals, 127
Ipomoea alba, 55
Ipomoea tricolor, 55
Irrigation. *See Watering*
Island beds, rectangular, 86–95

J

Joseph's-coat. *See Amaranthus
   tricolor*

K

Kale. *See Brassica oleracea*
Kochia scoparia, 56

L

Larkspur. *See Consolida ambigua*
Lathyrus coloratus, 56
Lavatera trimestris, 57
Lawns, 74
Limnanthes douglasii, 57

Limonium sinuatum, 59
Linaria maroccana, 59
Lisianthus russulanus, 60
Livingstone Daisy. *See Dorotheanus*
    bellidiformis
Lobelia erinus, 60
Lobularia maritima, 61
Lovely Browallia. *See Browallia sp.*
Low-growing annuals, 124

M

Machaeranthera tanacetifolia, 61
Marigold. *See Calendula officinalis;*
    Dimorphoteca sinuata; Tagetes
    erecta; Tagetes patula;
    Tagetes tenuifolia
Matthiola incana, 62
Meadow-foam. *See Limnanthes*
    douglasii
Medium-growing annuals, 124
Mexican Sunflower. *See Tithonia*
    rotundifolia
Mexican Tulip Poppy. *See Hunnemannia*
    fumariifolia
Mignonette. *See Reseda odorata*
Mimulus hybridus, 62
Mirabilis jalapa, 63
Moluccella laevis, 63
Monarch-of-the-veldt. *See Venidium*
    fastuosum

Monkey Flower. *See Mimulus hybridus*
Moonflower. *See Ipomoea alba*
Morning Glory. *See Ipomoea tricolor*
Moss Rose. *See Portulaca grandiflora*
Myosotis sylvatica, 64

N

Nasturtium. *See Tropaeolum majus*
Naturalizing annuals, 128
Nemesia strumosa, 64
Nemophila menziesii, 65
Nettle. *See Coleus hybrida*
Nicotiana alata, 65
Nierembergia hippomanica, 66
Nolana napiformis, 66

O

Orchid. *See Schizanthus wisetonensis*
Ornamental Cabbage. *See Brassica*
    oleracea
Ornamental Gourd. *See Cucurbita pepo*
Ornamental Kale. *See Brassica*
    oleracea
Ornamental Pepper. *See Capsicum*
    annuum

P

Painted Daisy. *See Chrysanthemum*
    carinatum

Painted Tongue. *See Salpiglossis*
    sinuata
Pansy. *See Viola tricolor*
Papaver nudicaule, 68
Papaver rhoeas, 68
Patience Plant. *See Impatiens*
    wallerana
Peat pellets, 14
Peat pots, 14
Peat seed trays, 14–17
Pelargonium hortorum, 69
Penstemon gloxinioides, 69
Pepper. *See Capsicum annuum*
Periwinkle. *See Catharanthus roseus*
Pests, 21
Petunia hybrida, 70
Phlox drummondii, 70
Pincushion Flower. *See Scabiosa*
    atropurpurea
Plastic pots, 14
Plastic seed trays, 14–17
Poor Man's Orchid. *See Schizanthus*
    wisetonensis
Poppy. *See Eschscholzia californica;*
    Hunnemannia fumariifolia;
    Papaver nudicaule; Papaver
    rhoeas
Portulaca grandiflora, 71
Pot-marigold. *See Calendula*
    officinalis
Pots, plastic, 14

Prairie Gentian. *See Lisianthus*
    russulanus
Preplanters, 14

R

Rainbow Daisy. *See Gazania rigens*
Raised beds, *20–21*
Reseda odorata, 71
Ricinus communis, 72
Rock gardens, 25
Rose. *See Portulaca grandiflora*
Rose-mallow. *See Lavatera trimestris*
Rudbeckia hirta burpeeii, 72

S

Sage. *See Salvia splendens*
Salpiglossis sinuata, 73
Salvia farinacea, 73
Salvia splendens, 75
Sanvitalia procumbens, 75
Satin Flower. *See Clarkia amoena*
Scabiosa atropurpurea, 76
Scabious. *See Scabiosa atropurpurea*
Scarlet Sage. *See Salvia splendens*
Schizanthus wisetonensis, 76
Scrambled Eggs. *See Limnanthes*
    douglasii

Seeds
germination, 13
starting techniques, 13–17
watering, 13
Seed tapes, 14
Seed trays, 14–17
Senecio cineraria, 77
Shade
annuals for, 127
sun vs., 19
Shirley Poppy. *See Papaver rhoeas*
Site selection, 19
Slugs, 21
Snapdragon. *See Antirrhinum majus*
Snow-on-the-mountain. *See Euphorbia marginata*
Soil
moist, 126
preparation of, 17–19
seed-starting and, 13–14
testing, 19
Southern Hibiscus. *See Hibiscus moscheutos*
Statice. *See Limonium sinuatum*
Stocks. *See Matthiola incana*
Strawflower. *See Helichrysum bracteatum*
Striped Marigold. *See Tagetes tenuifolia*

Summer Forget-me-not. *See Anchusa capensis*
Summer Verbena. *See Verbena hybrida*
Sun, shade vs., 19
Sunflower. *See Helianthus annuus; Tithonia rotundifolia*
Swan River Daisy. *See Brachycome iberidifolia*
Sweet Pea. *See Lathyrus coloratus*
Sweet Scabious. *See Scabiosa atropurpurea*

T

Tagetes erecta, 77
Tagetes patula, 78
Tagetes tenuifolia, 78
Tahoka-daisy. *See Machaeranthera tanacetifolia*
Tall-growing annuals, 125
Theme gardens, *8–9,* 10
Thunbergia alata, 79
Tithonia rotundifolia, 79
Toadflax. *See Linaria maroccana*
Tobacco. *See Nicotiana alata*
Torenia fournieri, 80
Transplanting, 13
pests and, 21
purchased plants for, 17
Tropaeolum majus, 80
Tulip Poppy. *See Hunnemannia fumariifolia*

V

Velvet Flower. *See Salpiglossis sinuata*
Venidium fastuosum, 81
Verbena hybrida, 81
Vinca. *See Catharanthus roseus*
Vining annuals, 131
Viola tricolor, 82

W

Water gardens, 25, *84–85*
Watering, 13, 19, *27*
Wax Begonia. *See Begonia semperflorens*
Weeding, 21
Williamsburg design, 96–105
Wishbone Flower. *See Torenia fournieri*

X

Xeranthemum annuum, 82

Z

Zinnia. *See Sanvitalia procumbens; Zinnia angustifolia; Zinnia elegans*
Zinnia angustifolia, 83
Zinnia elegans, 83